Preparing for the External Assessment

To be prepared for the external examination you must ensure that you are completely familiar with what the paper will require you to do.

The external assessment for Intermediate 2 Business Management is one paper with a duration of **one hour and 45 minutes**.

The paper is split into two sections:

- **Section One – Case study and questions**
- **Section Two – A choice of two from five Extended Response questions**

The paper is marked out of 75 marks.

Section One of the paper is worth 25 marks and is based on a case study. This section is **compulsory** and you must attempt all of the questions. The case study will be approximately 500 words in length. You must make sure that you read this carefully **before** attempting any questions. Not all answers will have to relate to the case study and questions can cover any of the topics from any parts of the Course.

Section Two of the question paper introduces some degree of choice. There are five questions, each worth 25 marks. You must answer two of these questions. The questions are integrated – this means that they will come from various parts of the Course thus making it impossible to pass by only revising certain parts of the Course.

It is very important that you read all five questions carefully before deciding on the two questions that you are going to attempt. Pay careful attention to the mark allocation for each part of the question and ensure that you answer the question that you feel you can achieve the most marks in.

Useful Tips

- When writing your answers to any question in this examination, it is essential that you **answer the question that is asked**.

- You may answer in bullet points where you are asked to 'identify, give, or name' points, but you must develop your answers where other command words are used.

- In some instances, the use of up-to-date examples may be credited.

- As a general rule **one correct point will equal one mark**, so if a question is worth five marks you most write five correct statements to get full marks.

- If a question asks for a diagram to be used then full marks will not be awarded unless one is supplied. All diagrams must contain a title and must be labelled appropriately. If you believe an answer would benefit from a diagram, do not be afraid to supply this as you may be given credit for it as part of description.

The Scottish Qualifications Authority (SQA) has issued a list of command words, which are used in Intermediate 2 Business Management to assist both teachers and candidates. Typically, every question contains a command word, around which your answer should be constructed. The list gives the meanings for the command words, which are used in the external assessment. It is essential that you make yourself familiar with these words, their meanings and how to answer questions in the examination. Your classroom teacher should be able to help you with this part of the examination technique. The list of command words follows.

Command word	Definition
Compare	Identify similarities and differences between two or more factors
Define	Give a clear meaning
Describe	Provide a thorough description
Distinguish	Identify the differences between two or more factors
Explain	Give details about how and why something is as it is
Give	Pick some key factors and name them
Identify	Give the name or identifying characteristics of something
Name	Identify or make a list
Outline	State the main features
Suggest	State a possible reason or course of action (no development required)

Good luck – we hope you find the book helpful and that you achieve success in the Intermediate 2 examination.

INTERMEDIATE 2

Business Management
Case Studies and Exam Preparation

Phyllis Macleod
Kirsty MacPherson
Shelley Thomson

Consultant: Alistair Wylie

HODDER
GIBSON
PART OF HACHETTE LIVRE UK

The Publishers would like to thank the following for permission to reproduce copyright material:

Photo credits
Page 2 Image courtesy of The Herald & Evening Times picture archive; page 5 Picture courtesy of Shell UK Ltd and Shell Livewire; page 6 © Brian Sweeney/Guardian News & Media Ltd 2007; page 8 © Justin Kase zfourz/Alamy; page 11 © JUPITERIMAGES/Brand X/Alamy; page 12 © Jon Beretta/Carl Sims/Rex Features; page 14 © Daniel Allan/Taxi/Getty Images; page 17 (top) © ICP/Alamy, (bottom) © Cris Haigh/Alamy; page 20 © Tim Hill/Alamy; page 23 (top) © Juniors Bildarchiv/Alamy, (bottom) © Kevin Foy/Alamy; page 26 © Tracy Hebden/Alamy; page 29 © JUPITERIMAGES/ BananaStock/Alamy; page 32 © JUPITERIMAGES/ Comstock Images/Alamy; page 35 With kind permission of Fraser Doherty; page 36 With kind permission of Fraser Doherty; page 38 With kind permission of Fifi and Ally; page 39 Image courtesy of The Herald & Evening Times picture archive; page 41 © image100/Corbis; page 42 © Neil McAllister/Alamy; page 44 Organic Picture Library/Rex Features; page 45 © Patrick Eden/Alamy.

Acknowledgements
'Top deli wants bigger slice of city business' by Caroline Wilson, Reproduced with the permission of The Evening Times, Glasgow © 2008 Herald & Times Group; 'Customising shoes for the stars' copyright Guardian News and Media Ltd 2007; 'Ikea feels the pinch as High Street sales hit retail parks' copyright Daily Mail 2007; 'Kids' clothes designers target Russia with style' by Jonathan Rennie, Reproduced with the permission of The Evening Times, Glasgow © 2008 Herald & Times Group; 'SuperJam' article from Strathclyde People magazine is reproduced by permission of the University of Strathclyde; 'Fifi and Ally set to open London store' by Marianne Taylor, Reproduced with the permission of The Evening Times, Glasgow © 2008 Herald & Times Group.

Every effort has been made to trace all copyright holders, but if any have been inadvertently overlooked the Publishers will be pleased to make the necessary arrangements at the first opportunity.

Although every effort has been made to ensure that website addresses are correct at time of going to press, Hodder Gibson cannot be held responsible for the content of any website mentioned in this book. It is sometimes possible to find a relocated web page by typing in the address of the home page for a website in the URL window of your browser.

Hachette's policy is to use papers that are natural, renewable and recyclable products and made from wood grown in sustainable forests. The logging and manufacturing processes are expected to conform to the environmental regulations of the country of origin.

Orders: please contact Bookpoint Ltd, 130 Milton Park, Abingdon, Oxon OX14 4SB. Telephone: (44) 01235 827720. Fax: (44) 01235 400454. Lines are open 9.00 – 5.00, Monday to Saturday, with a 24-hour message answering service. Visit our website at www.hoddereducation.co.uk. Hodder Gibson can be contacted direct on: Tel: 0141 848 1609; Fax: 0141 889 6315; email: hoddergibson@hodder.co.uk

© Phyllis Macleod, Kirsty MacPherson and Shelley Thomson 2008
First published in 2008 by
Hodder Gibson, an imprint of Hodder Education,
An Hachette Livre UK Company,
2a Christie Street
Paisley PA1 1NB

Impression number	5	4	3	2	1
Year	2012	2011	2010	2009	2008

Cover photo © Zoran Vukmanov Simokov/iStockphoto.com
Illustrations by Fakenham Photosetting Limited
Typeset in 10.5/13pt ITC Century Std Light by Fakenham Photosetting Limited
Printed in Great Britain by Martins The Printers, Berwick-upon-Tweed

A catalogue record for this title is available from the British Library

ISBN-13: 978 0340 965 207

CONTENTS

Introduction

Welcome to Intermediate 2 Business Management Case Studies and Exam Preparation. It has been written in such a way that it will be useful in both a classroom environment and as a self-study tool to allow you to prepare for the SQA Intermediate 2 level examination in Business Management.

The authors are experienced educators in the secondary education sector and all have many years experience of marking Business Management at Higher, Intermediate 2 and Intermediate 1 levels.

The book comprises 15 case studies set to the standard of Section One of the Intermediate 2 level external assessment and 45 questions set to the standard of Section Two of the Intermediate 2 level external assessment. There are also suggested outline answers to case studies and questions and useful tips for exam preparation and coverage of the construction of the external paper.

The book is divided into four sections:

- **Tips on examination preparation and the construction of the exam paper**
- **Section One Case Studies and Questions**
- **Section Two Questions**
- **Suggested solutions to all case studies and questions**

It should be noted that suggested solutions to all case studies and questions are provided in an abbreviated format and are not exhaustive in nature. Other answers may be acceptable in addition to those suggested. The answers provided give a summary of some of the main points that the authors believe should be contained in a good answer and are given in a bulleted format for ease of reference. The command word used in each question should also be reflected and given due consideration in the answer. Note that this is not covered in the abbreviated format solutions.

We are indebted to our families for their patience during the writing of this book and to our friends, colleagues and peers for their advice and encouragement in its preparation. Special thanks must also go to the staff at Hodder Gibson, Paisley, in particular John Mitchell and Katherine Bennett for their support for the book.

We, the authors, hope that you will find this a useful resource during your period of study and preparation for external examination in the subject.

Phyllis Macleod
Kirsty MacPherson
Shelley Thomson

SECTION ONE

Case Studies

Garlic

This section should take you approximately 45 minutes. Read the following information, then answer the questions which follow.

BACKGROUND

The Eusebi family opened a small family-run delicatessen in Shettleston – one of the most deprived areas of Glasgow – selling freshly cooked Italian food, wine, sauces and cheese. The deli – named *Garlic* – offers quality food cheaper than the price of a fish supper, in an area where the average life expectancy for men is just 64 years old. Edmund Eusebi said, 'We want to bring the authentic Italian deli back to Glasgow. Everything we stock has come from small independent retailers across the UK and Europe. All the food is affordable and everything is freshly cooked.'

CURRENT SITUATION

Garlic has been a huge success in the Shettleston outlet in the heart of the East End of Glasgow. The Eusebi family are keen to extend this success to a new branch in the West End of Glasgow and have just been granted planning permission for an outlet on Gibson Street, near Glasgow University. This new store will include an Italian food hall, café, ice cream parlour and basement cooking area.

In order to staff this new store, the Eusebi family will need to undertake a recruitment campaign. Giovanna Eusebi, pictured above, will be involved in drawing up the recruitment pack for all the jobs on offer. Getting the right staff for this venture is very important as the Eusebi family want Garlic to be seen as a high-quality deli.

In order to keep the authenticity of the food, the Eusebi family continually source food from Europe. With an increasing demand for healthy eating, they must keep this in mind when placing orders with their suppliers. ICT is a great aid to businesses who wish to source quality supplies from abroad. However, although Garlic use ICT to aid their business, they have yet to use it to set up their own website.

Glasgow city centre is also home to another popular deli – Peckhams. This provides competition for Garlic, but the Eusebi family are keen to offer their customers something a little different. In view of the success of TV programmes such as Gordon Ramsay's *Kitchen Nightmares* and *Celebrity Chef*, Giovanna is contemplating offering short cooking courses in the basement cooking area of their new branch. They are keen to take advantage of the recent hype about learning to cook and believe they have the necessary skills and talents to offer these courses.

OPTIONS FOR THE FUTURE

Option 1   Specialise in healthy food only.

Option 2   Set up a website for the business.

Option 3   Open up the basement for cooking courses.

The Eusebi family may choose options 2 and 3.

Adapted from: Caroline Wilson, 'Top deli wants bigger slice of city business', *Evening Times*, 23 April 2007

QUESTIONS

Marks

1   (a)   Garlic will need to recruit new staff to work in their new branch. **4**
Describe the selection process Giovanna is likely to use to ensure they get the right candidates for the job.

(b)   Identify and describe the training the Eusebi family may offer to these **2** new recruits.

2   Garlic have chosen to open a new branch in order to grow.

(a)   Describe 3 reasons why an organisation may choose to grow. **3**

(b)   Describe 3 methods of growth. **3**

3   The Eusebi family have chosen options 2 and 3.

    (a)   Explain why they may have chosen option 2.   **1**

    (b)   Explain why they may have chosen option 3.   **1**

    (c)   Explain why they may not have chosen option 1.   **1**

4   Since the business is growing quickly, the Eusebi family may need to   **4**
organise their business and staff around certain groupings. Identify and
describe 2 types of groupings that may suit this type of business.

5   Most organisations in today's society make a lot of use of ICT.

    (a)   Excluding the internet, describe 2 pieces of ICT that businesses   **2**
find helpful.

    (b)   Other than the financial cost of the ICT, describe 2 costs and   **4**
2 benefits that ICT brings to organisations.

(25)

CASE STUDIES

Star Sparkles

This section should take you approximately 45 minutes. Read the following information, then answer the questions which follow.

Fashion icon Paris Hilton has an army of designers queuing up to get her to wear their clothes, but enterprising Pauline Clifford took matters into her own hands when she flew out to Beverly Hills to personally deliver a free pair of her glitzy shoes to the millionaire heiress. Miss Hilton was spotted wearing these customised trainers days later in Los Angeles.

Pauline was runner-up in Scotland's Shell LiveWIRE Young Entrepreneur of the Year 2007.

BACKGROUND

Pauline worked in Sir Tom Hunter's Qube shoe shop in Glasgow's Buchanan Galleries when she first got the idea for *Star Sparkles*. Her big break came when she customised some Adidas and Puma trainers for her boss, Gerry Gray, using Swarovski crystals.

Pauline had originally planned to do this as a hobby but her designs soon attracted lots of attention and Pauline was asked to produce more trainers for other designers. Pauline felt there was a gap in the market for these products and decided to set up a business selling her blingtastic trainers. She received help from the Prince's Scottish Youth Business Trust to get her business off the ground. These customised trainers are only available through her Star Sparkles website www.starsparkles.com or via Qube shoe shop.

CURRENT SITUATION

Demand for Pauline's trainers continues to rise and, despite her trainers being priced at the higher end of the trainer market, many pairs fly off the shelves every week. Pauline may find it difficult to keep up with such demand and may need to advertise for designers to work on orders and

CASE STUDIES

support her in the business. Pauline is keen to ensure that she keeps up with demand to avoid getting any bad publicity.

Pauline has been approached by upmarket department stores such as Selfridges and Harvey Nichols, and high-street chains such as Office. These stores are keen to stock Pauline's pre-customised shoes and are talking about selling these on at £180–200 per pair.

Pauline really enjoys running her own business, but realises the decisions she makes now will have a big impact on her future.

OPTIONS FOR THE FUTURE

Pauline may consider the following options:

Option 1   Sign a deal with the upmarket department stores and the high-street chain Office.

Option 2   Open a shop herself to sell her designs.

Option 3   Retain her internet site and continue selling online.

Pauline may choose options 1 and 3.

Adapted from: 'Customising shoes for the stars', *The Guardian*, 30 March 2007, copyright Guardian News and Media Ltd 2007

QUESTIONS

Marks

1   Identify two areas of strength for Pauline's business and explain why each success is a benefit for Pauline.   **4**

2   (a)   Pauline is a sole trader. Describe this type of business organisation.   **1**

    (b)   Identify and describe 2 other types of business organisations.   **4**

3   Pauline may choose options 1 and 3.

    (a)   Give one reason why Pauline may choose option 1.   **1**

    (b)   Give one reason why Pauline may choose option 3.   **1**

    (c)   Give one reason why Pauline may not choose option 2.   **1**

4 Many businesses choose to sell online. Other than selling online, describe 2 advantages to a business of setting up a website.　　**2**

5 Pauline may have to advertise for members of staff. Explain the difference between the following two terms:　　**2**

● internal recruitment

● external recruitment

6 (a) Pauline chose to give Paris Hilton a free pair of her designer trainers. Identify the term which would describe this marketing technique.　　**1**

(b) Explain the benefit of this marketing technique.　　**1**

7 Star Sparkles is a company in the growth stage of the product life cycle. Describe 2 other stages and illustrate all 4 stages by means of a diagram.　　**5**

8 If the business grows, Pauline may have to organise it into functional departments. Describe the main role of the following functional departments:　　**2**

● operations

● finance

(25)

CASE STUDIES

Growing Pains

This section should take you approximately 45 minutes. Read the following information, then answer the questions which follow.

BACKGROUND

Sam Brown opened his garden centre three years ago. He and his wife Amy formed a partnership. The business is situated on the outskirts of a busy town and has proved very popular. Sam and his staff grow many of the plants from seed, but Sam also buys in plants from a number of suppliers. Sam and Amy have eight members of staff – five work full-time and three work part-time. The part-time staff are responsible for looking after the shop within the garden centre. The shop stocks dairy produce, stationery, books and small gifts. During the summer months the garden centre is extremely busy.

CURRENT SITUATION

Sam and Amy are keen to expand the business. They have decided that the introduction of a tearoom would be a good way to do this. To fund this expansion, they will need to borrow money. They will also need to employ staff to run the tearoom. Both Sam and Amy feel a tearoom will enhance their business and also increase profits.

OPTIONS FOR THE FUTURE

Sam has consulted a firm of architects who have drawn up plans for the tearoom. They have outlined three options.

Option 1   Construct a tearoom on the upper floor of the premises with an attractive stairway leading up to it. A tearoom on the upper floor

would allow for 20 tables and chairs and a good-sized area for cooking. The architects have told Sam that this conversion could be done fairly easily at a reasonable cost.

Option 2   Construct a tearoom inside the gift shop. This would allow for nine tables and chairs. Customers would have easy access to it but it would mean that the gift shop would be much smaller as a result. However, a tearoom within the gift shop might attract more customers. The cost of erecting the tearoom in the gift shop would also be quite reasonable.

Option 3   Build a tearoom on part of the car park. This would allow for 40 tables and chairs and a good-sized area for cooking. Using part of the car park would mean that less parking would be available. It would be quite costly to erect a new building for the tearoom. However, it would mean that many more people could be accommodated. Amy is keen to have a completely different building for the tearoom as she feels it would give them a lot more scope. Sam is a bit apprehensive because of the cost.

After giving the matter a lot of consideration, Sam and Amy have decided that option 1 would be best.

QUESTIONS

Marks

1   Sam and Amy have chosen option 1. Explain 2 reasons why they may have decided on this option instead of option 2.   **2**

2   Sam uses suppliers for some of his plants and merchandise. Describe 4 factors he will look for in a good supplier.   **4**

3   Sam and Amy will require new staff for the tearoom. Describe how they could recruit new staff.   **4**

4   This business is a partnership. Describe 2 advantages and 2 disadvantages of a partnership.   **4**

5   Sam and Amy may apply for a bank loan or a grant to finance the extension.

   (a) Explain the difference between a grant and a bank loan.   **2**

   (b) Name 2 organisations that provide grants to businesses.   **2**

6   The garden centre is busier in the summer months. Describe marketing activities that could be used during the winter months to increase sales.   **2**

7   Sam and Amy will need to let people know about the tearoom. Describe   **3**
    3 methods they could use to do this.

8   Sam and Amy will be required to take account of the Health and Safety   **2**
    at Work Act. Explain how this Act affects both an employer and
    employees.

(25)

Cuppa Chino

This section should take you approximately 45 minutes. Read the following information, then answer the questions which follow.

BACKGROUND

In January 2006, Tamara Brown had a small win on the National Lottery. She was shocked and could not believe her luck! It was not enough money to enable her to live a celebrity lifestyle but just enough to enable her to pay off her mortgage and quit her job as a junior accountant with the local council. After paying off her debts she was left with £20,000. She decided

to approach her local business gateway to get some advice on starting up her own coffee shop in Troon, a small town in the west of Scotland. This is an area that Tamara knows well and it attracts many tourists all year round. It is also an area famous for its golf courses.

After about 6 months of carrying out in-depth field and desk research Tamara completed a business plan. It covered: who her target market was, how much finance would be required to start the business, what equipment would be required and a cash flow statement for the first six months. Tamara completed a course in food hygiene where she learned about the preparation, processing, packaging, handling and storage of food. She also signed a three-year lease on suitable premises.

Tamara did not want her coffee shop to be the same as the other two competitors in town. She wanted to have a unique selling point (USP) that would attract people to her business. She decided to install a small soft-play area where children up to the age of 5 could play and let their mums and dads relax and enjoy their cuppa.

In December 2006 with the help of two full-time employees Tamara opened the shop to the public. She kept her menu simple yet contemporary. Her luscious lattes and tasty teas were an instant hit and, because of the time of year, she was exceptionally busy with Christmas shoppers looking to rest their weary feet and enjoy a bite to eat.

CURRENT SITUATION

In January 2007, the sales revenue for the shop had halved but Tamara was not unduly concerned and thought it might just be the time of the year and the novelty of her new shop wearing thin.

By March, there did not seem to be any sign of improvement and Tamara had to let one of her full-time employees go. She was very concerned by the downturn and knew that it was crucial to gain a good hold on the market in the first year of business. She was determined not to let her dream turn into a nightmare. Tamara went to see her business advisor at the Small Business Gateway to obtain advice on retaining and attracting clients. They discussed the following options.

OPTIONS FOR THE FUTURE

Option 1   Begin an advertising campaign.

Option 2   Introduce promotions.

Option 3   Introduce new services such as children's parties.

Option 4   Take on a partner.

Tamara chose options 1, 2 and 3.

QUESTIONS

		Marks
1	Identify 2 strengths of Tamara's business.	**2**
2	From the options for the future Tamara chose options 1, 2 and 3.	
	(a) Give one reason to explain why she chose option 1.	**1**
	(b) Identify and justify 2 types of promotions (other than advertising) that the business may use.	**4**
	(c) Give 2 reasons why Tamara did not choose option 4.	**2**
3	Tamara had a three-year lease on her premises.	
	Describe the difference between a lease and a mortgage.	**2**
4	Customers, the environmental health department and employees are stakeholders in Tamara's business.	
	(a) Describe the influence of each of these stakeholders on Tamara's business.	**3**
	(b) Describe the impact on Tamara's business of each of these stakeholders.	**3**
5	Tamara's sales revenue dropped.	
	(a) Describe the effect that this would have on the Trading Profit and Loss Account and the Balance Sheet.	**2**
	(b) Describe the purpose of preparing a cash flow statement.	**2**
6	(a) Distinguish between field and desk research.	**2**
	(b) Give an example of each.	**2**
		(25)

IKEA

This section should take you approximately 45 minutes. Read the following information then answer the questions which follow.

BACKGROUND

Ikea opened its first store in Sweden in 1958 and now has numerous stores throughout the world. One main objective of Ikea is to offer a wide range of home furnishings of good design at low prices so that as many people as possible can afford to buy them. Ikea has been very popular with British customers. Most of Ikea's stores are situated in retail parks which, until recently, customers appeared to find convenient.

CURRENT SITUATION

Difficult market conditions have hit retail parks. This has resulted in lower sales for Ikea whose profits in British stores have fallen in the past year.

One reason for this is that other stores such as Asda, Tesco and Marks and Spencer have introduced a wide range of home furnishings. These organisations have refurbished many of their High Street stores and are now able to display a wide range of furniture and furnishings. They have also introduced home shopping catalogues which customers can pick up from the store while doing their weekly shopping. According to Tesco, their catalogue sales are booming.

Ikea has a tall management structure. There are many senior management posts throughout the organisation.

The Head of operations in the UK recently carried out market research. Feedback from customers revealed that they would like to see more staff on the shop floor to advise and consult them about products. Another

complaint was that too few checkouts were in operation resulting in long queues.

Ikea are keen to remain competitive. To do this they have been looking into offering pre-fabricated houses for sale at reasonable prices. They are aware that first time buyers are finding it difficult to get onto the housing market.

In order to deal with their present problems the following options are open to them.

OPTIONS FOR THE FUTURE

Option 1   Change the structure of the business from a tall structure to a flat structure and introduce more sales advisors and supervisors.

Option 2   Go ahead with plans to introduce prefabricated homes for sale.

Option 3   Keep the present management structure and remain as they are.

Option 4   Send out their home shopping catalogue to a wider range of people and introduce special offers.

Ikea may decide to choose options 1, 2 and 4 in order to remain competitive.

Adapted from: 'Ikea feels the pinch as High Street sales hit retail parks', *Daily Mail*, 11 July 2007

QUESTIONS

Marks

1   Ikea may decide to change its organisation structure.   **2**

   (a)   Describe the following types of organisation structure:

   ● flat structure

   ● tall structure

   (b)   If Ikea changes its structure, managers will have a wider span of control. Explain the term "wide span of control".   **1**

2   Ikea carried out market research. Identify and describe 3 methods they may have used to carry out this research.   **6**

3   Ikea expect to employ more sales staff. Describe the recruitment and selection process used by organisations.   **6**

4 Explain 2 reasons why Ikea has suffered falling profits. **4**

5 Describe 3 objectives of Ikea. **3**

6 Explain how each of the following stakeholders could have an influence on Ikea: **3**

- Government
- Customers
- Suppliers

(25)

Scottish Signs

This section should take you approximately 45 minutes. Read the following information, then answer the questions which follow.

BACKGROUND

John Flynn wanted to be his own boss and to provide a stable future for his family. He had taken part in an apprenticeship with a local sign writing business and completed a course at college in sign writing. In 1973, he opened a small workshop on the outskirts of Aberdeen. *Scottish Signs* design, manufacture and install various types of signage. John's main areas of expertise lay in lettering vans and making signs for shops. Other services include printing banners, health and safety signs and window graphics.

As Scottish Signs grew, John's wife Jenny joined the business. She had been made redundant from her administration post at a local company. She contributed some capital to the business, and John and Jenny became business partners. Jenny's main role was to help retain and attract clients and deal with the many office tasks. This included dealing with clients, answering the telephone and doing the accounts.

Over the years Jenny's job evolved and she showed a real understanding and flair for sign writing. Jenny recognised that signage was an important marketing tool for any business and if the signs were well-designed and constructed their business would grow. Jenny decided the business should recruit two members of staff to be

sign fitters; this would free up both her and John's time to dedicate to the design and manufacture of the signage. They wanted to continue to keep their business small- to medium-sized, as they believed that clients preferred a friendly and personal service.

John and Jenny invested a large sum of capital to update their equipment to include some of the latest digital technology to help manufacture the signs.

CURRENT SITUATION

After 30 years, John and Jenny are looking to retire and enjoy a quiet life on the Costa Brava. They have worked very hard and they are worried about the continued success of the business. They also want to ensure the job security of the loyal shop fitters that have worked for the business for the past 15 years. They are well-trained and have considerable experience in sign writing. One of the workers has expressed an interest in becoming more involved in the management of the business.

The Flynn's only daughter, Holly, is not interested in taking on the business as she specialises in media studies. She is keen for her parents to sell the business.

A competitor in the area has offered John and Jenny a very generous sum to buy them out of their business.

OPTIONS FOR THE FUTURE

Option 1   Promote one of their employees to manager to run the business on their behalf.

Option 2   Employ an experienced manager to run the business.

Option 3   Sell the business to the rival sign writing company.

Option 4   Delay retirement.

After a great deal of consideration John and Jenny have decided to choose option 1.

QUESTIONS

Marks

1   The capital that Jenny contributed was recorded in a **partnership agreement**.

(a)   Describe the purpose of this agreement.   1

(b)   State 2 other items that would appear within the document.   2

2 John and Jenny chose option 1.

    (a) Give one advantage of choosing option 1.   **1**

    (b) Give one disadvantage of choosing option 1.   **1**

    (c) Give one reason why they may not have chosen option 2.   **1**

3 Option 3 was a method of horizontal integration.

Describe 3 **other** methods of growth.   **3**

4 Scottish Signs used equipment in the manufacture of their products.

Suggest 2 advantages and 2 disadvantages of using equipment in the production of goods and services.   **4**

5 The shop fitters are stakeholders in Scottish Signs and their main interest is job security.

    (a) Describe 2 influences that the shop fitters may have on the business.   **2**

    (b) Identify 2 other stakeholders and describe their interest in the business.   **4**

6 (a) John attended college to enhance his sign writing skills.

        (i) Name this type of training.   **1**

        (ii) Describe one other method of training.   **1**

    (b) Describe 2 costs and 2 benefits of staff training.   **4**

                                          (25)

CASE STUDIES

Healthy Options

This section should take you approximately 45 minutes. Read the following information, then answer the questions which follow.

BACKGROUND

Adam and Anna Miller started up their business *Healthy Options* in 2001. They were convinced that there was a gap in the market for good healthy food at reasonable prices. They studied the fast-food market and carried out market research. They found that most rival firms tended to supply sandwiches, burgers and fizzy drinks, whereas they were interested in supplying something different such as baguettes and paninis containing healthy fillings. Healthy smoothies containing juice from fresh fruit were also on their menu. One of their main objectives was to sell food that would be of the highest quality.

Adam and Anna had formerly managed a restaurant for one of the big fast-food chains so they had a lot of experience in preparing and buying food. They also knew how to manage a business.

With most of their savings and a mortgage on their house as security, they opened their first shop in Glasgow. It proved very successful. Many firms placed daily orders for their staff. In order to keep up with the demand they had to employ two assistants to help them make up the orders and sell behind the counter. Owing to the success of their first shop, Adam and Anna decided to open another two shops.

In 2003 one of their shops suffered flood damage. It took three months for the shop to re-open. The closure of the shop resulted in cash flow problems for Adam and Anna. This was a learning experience for them and with careful planning they were able to survive.

CURRENT SITUATION

Adam and Anna now have 15 shops. Life has become very hectic. Although they employ managers in each of their shops, they still like to spend time in each shop to ensure that quality standards and health and safety regulations are complied with. They are careful when they have to recruit new staff as they want the business to maintain its high profile of good service and healthy options.

Adam and Anna feel that they do not have enough time to run the overall business and develop it further. They are keen to expand, widen their product range and make their business a household name. To do this, they are considering the following options:

OPTIONS FOR THE FUTURE

Option 1   Take on a partner.

Option 2   Allow people to buy shares in their business and become a PLC.

Option 3   Allow franchisees to run their shops.

After careful consideration, Adam and Anna have chosen option 3.

QUESTIONS

Marks

1   Healthy Options is to be run as a franchise.

   (a) Define the term 'franchise'.   **1**

   (b) Explain one advantage and one disadvantage for the franchisee.   **2**

2   Adam and Anna used their home as security when starting their business.

   (a) Describe 2 other sources they could have used to obtain finance.   **2**

   (b) Describe one advantage and one disadvantage of **each** source you have described above.   **4**

3   Adam and Anna have made a strategic decision to allow franchisees to run their shops. Describe the decision making process.   **5**

4   Adam and Anna experienced cash flow problems when flooding damaged one of their shops. Describe 4 methods that organisations can use to resolve cash flow problems.   **4**

5   Adam and Anna are very selective when recruiting staff. Describe the   **4**
recruitment process.

6   Flooding was an external factor that affected one of the shops. Describe   **3**
3 other external factors that can affect businesses.

(25)

Perfect Paws

This section should take you approximately 45 minutes. Read the following information, then answer the questions which follow.

BACKGROUND

Nicola Jones loves all kinds of animals, but dogs hold a special place in her affections. As a child she spent hours grooming her West Highland terrier. She also attended classes and holds certificates in dog grooming. Nicola trained as a Veterinary Nurse because of her interest in animals and she worked at a Veterinary Hospital for five years. She also did some dog grooming for friends in her spare time.

As more and more people approached Nicola to groom their dogs, she decided to open a business offering her services. With a grant from her local enterprise trust and her savings she was able to buy a second-hand van to allow her to travel to clients' houses to carry out her services. These services include shampooing, brushing, nail clipping and ear and eye cleaning.

CURRENT SITUATION

Nicola is surprised at how popular her services have become and finds she is working flat out most days. She also covers a lot of mileage in her van. Recently her van broke down and she had to hire another one to allow her to continue working. This proved to be quite expensive on top of the garage bill she had to pay to

repair her van. However, the profits she has made in the past two years have far exceeded her expectations and she has a very healthy bank balance.

Since she opened her business two years ago, Nicola has not had a holiday and has had few days off. Many of her friends get annoyed when she does not go out with them at the weekend. Nicola is either working or too exhausted to socialise. Nicola's mum is always getting on to her – she feels her 22-year-old daughter should be enjoying life instead of constantly working.

Boarding kennels situated near Nicola often ask her to groom dogs for their customers and, rather than let them down, Nicola has had to employ a nurse from the Vet Hospital to help her out.

A vet's practice has recently opened up nearby and the owner has asked Nicola if she would like to rent a room in his premises to carry out her business. The vet sees opportunities in this for both of them. Nicola does not want to lose any of the clients that she visits nor her contact with the boarding kennels. However, the offer from the vet is very tempting.

OPTIONS FOR THE FUTURE

Nicola now has the following options:

Option 1   Continue to offer the mobile service.

Option 2   Accept the vet's offer to rent a room.

Option 3   Employ the nurse on a permanent basis.

Nicola has chosen all of the above options.

QUESTIONS

Marks

1   Nicola has chosen all 3 options. Explain why she has chosen each of the options. (You should refer to all the options in your answer.)   **3**

2   Nicola operates as a sole trader. Identify and describe 3 other types of business organisations.   **6**

3   The nurse who helps Nicola is employed on a temporary basis. Describe the following types of employment: **3**

● temporary

● part-time

● full-time

4 Explain 2 advantages for the vet when Nicola rents a room in his premises. **2**

5 Nicola received a grant from her local enterprise trust and used her savings to start her business.

 Identify 2 other sources from which she could have obtained finance to start her business and give a disadvantage of each source. **4**

6 Name and describe 2 pieces of legislation that Nicola will be required to take into account in the course of her business. **4**

7 Describe 3 pieces of ICT that Nicola could use in her business. **3**

 (25)

Soft and Pure Skin Solutions

This section should take you approximately 45 minutes. Read the following information, then answer the questions which follow.

BACKGROUND

The skin and beauty industry is a growing market. This is mainly due to high-profile celebrities' interest in looking good and stopping the ageing process.

In 2005 a group of like-minded chemistry graduates spotted a gap in the market and launched *Soft and Pure Skin Solutions Ltd*. The original business idea came from their interest in natural medicine approaches and from their friend Sally, who was an aromatherapist. Sally used many products in her line of business but she was aware of a lack of pure and natural products that worked.

The group developed a range of natural skin care products aimed at women. They were aware that everyone had different skin types: from oily to dry or even mixed. This meant that they had to develop products that were aimed at each of the main skin types. Their first range of products included face creams, shampoos and bath oils. They also produced a range of baby products that are gentle to the skin.

Each one of their products starts with research about the skin type and this knowledge is used to identify the right combination of unique and natural ingredients to make the product. The focus on natural and pure ingredients ensures that they stand out from their competitors. They do not use added chemicals or colourings. None of the products are tested on animals. Their experience in science, along with Sally's experience in aromatherapy, has helped them to develop the brand.

In first setting up, they sold their products through their own website. This helped them build up their business with minimal costs. They sent free

samples of their products to the local TV stations and to several of the main women's magazines. It was the review of the product in a magazine that gained them the publicity they needed to allow their products to grow and become more successful.

CURRENT SITUATION

In December 2007, a national chain store approached them wishing to stock their products. They decided that this was a good idea and have been pleased by the response of the public to their products and the exposure that they have been getting in the media. They were also recently short listed at a Green Business Award Ceremony.

However, they have now grown so big that they need to restructure the organisation and employ more staff to cope with the level of demand. They moved to a larger manufacturing plant so that they could cope with the scale of production that was going to be required.

They also wanted to look at how they could reach more people through marketing and public relations but since they were mainly scientists they did not have the necessary expertise in this area.

OPTIONS FOR THE FUTURE

Soft and Pure Skin Solutions Ltd have considered the following options:

Option 1   Become a PLC.

Option 2   Become a franchise.

Option 3   Launch a male grooming range.

Option 4   Employ a Marketing Director.

They chose options 1 and 4.

QUESTIONS

Marks

1   Soft and Pure Skin Solutions Ltd chose option 1.

   (a)   Explain how becoming a PLC will change Soft and Pure Skin Solutions.   **1**

   (b)   Describe 2 differences between a PLC and a limited company.   **2**

2   Option 4 was to employ a Marketing Director.

    (a)   Describe the possible role a Marketing Director could have in the business.   **2**

    (b)   Describe how the best candidate might be chosen for this role in the business.   **5**

3   Explain why the company did not choose option 2.   **1**

4   (a)   Describe 2 possible advantages of launching a male grooming range.   **2**

    (b)   State 2 reasons why a business would segment its market.   **2**

5   (a)   Identify a suitable type of production for the company's products and justify your choice.   **2**

    (b)   (i)   Identify one other type of production.   **1**

        (ii)   Explain 2 advantages and 2 disadvantages of the type of production identified in (b)(i).   **4**

6   (a)   Describe the purpose of research and development.   **2**

    (b)   Describe the significance of being nominated for a Green Business Award.   **1**

(25)

CASE STUDIES

Ollie Clothing

This section should take you approximately 45 minutes. Read the following information, then answer the questions which follow.

BACKGROUND

Ollie Clothing is based in Bridgeton in Glasgow and is run by husband and wife team Michael and Jennifer McGonigle. Michael and Jennifer set up the business in the year 2000 to provide streetwear for boys. The McGonigles believed that there was a gap in the market for trendy boys' clothes and tried to fill this gap by producing fashionable clothes for boys aged between 3 and 15 years old.

CURRENT SITUATION

Ollie Clothing has been a success and has secured contracts with large department stores such as Selfridges (London) and John Lewis. Michael, however, feels that the opportunity for growth in the UK is now limited to small, independent clothes retailers and this means there is little opportunity for them to grow. Ollie Clothing has therefore been looking to take their brand overseas and distribute in Germany, Italy and the Netherlands. However, the biggest opportunity available to them is to begin trading in Russia. Russia and India have seen a large growth in the fashion industry market in the last few years. Market research has shown that this overseas trade could lead to a 40–50% increase in business and profits.

Although Ollie Clothing is selling its products alongside brands such as Diesel, there has been a huge increase in the designer market for children, with Armani and Hugo Boss both producing a range of designer clothes for children. This undoubtedly creates competition for Ollie Clothing. These companies all specialise in high-quality, fashionable clothing for boys, but

also have a range for girls. Michael and Jennifer are keen to respond to this and are considering launching a range of clothing for girls.

An issue for customers of Ollie Clothing is that the business does not have a website. If customers try to search for Ollie Clothing they are disappointed that the search does not provide them with a website where they can look at products and buy online.

With growth a primary objective for Ollie Clothing, Michael and Jennifer may need to consider funding for any new venture. Michael and Jennifer could have chosen to float on the stock exchange to fund any future ventures, but at present they have decided to seek other sources of finance for their growth plans.

Remaining a small, UK-based company is not an option for Ollie Clothing.

OPTIONS FOR THE FUTURE

Michael and Jennifer are considering the following opportunities for the future of their business:

Option 1   Enter the Russian market.

Option 2   Produce a range of clothes for girls.

Option 3   Set up a website and sell online.

Michael and Jennifer may choose to implement all three options for the future.

Adapted from: Jonathan Rennie, 'Kids' clothes designers target Russia with style', *Evening Times*, **11 January 2007**

QUESTIONS

Marks

1   Michael and Jennifer have established Ollie Clothing as a brand name.   **3**
Describe 3 advantages of holding a brand name for a business.

2   (a)   Michael and Jennifer may choose to implement all 3 options for   **3**
the future. Explain why they may choose to implement each
option. You should provide a different reason for each option.

   (b)   Each option is an example of growth. Identify and describe 3   **6**
methods of growth that a company may choose to implement.

   (c)   Michael and Jennifer are not keen to float on the stock exchange to   **4**
gain additional finance. Describe 4 other sources of finance
that may be available to fund their growth plans.

3 (a) Identify and describe 2 methods Ollie Clothing could use to promote their online sales. **4**

(b) Compare the costs of setting up a website to those of setting up a store. Your answer should make reference to human resource costs and running expenses. **2**

4 Ollie Clothing makes use of batch production. Explain this term and describe 3 other types of production system. **3**

(25)

Clean4me

This section should take you approximately 45 minutes. Read the following information, then answer the questions which follow.

BACKGROUND

Divya and Dev had been friends for many years and they were both stunned when they were made redundant from their jobs as cleaners at the local primary school. The school decided to outsource their cleaning to a contract cleaning company. Divya and Dev saw this as an opportunity to run their own business and make an income, so they created their partnership *Clean4me*.

Divya and Dev started from humble beginnings. They used all their redundancy money to buy a small van and cleaning equipment, including vacuum cleaners, floor polishers and chemicals. They realised that in this early stage of their business they could not afford to rent premises so they decided to operate from Divya's spare room.

To begin with they focused on offering services like hoovering, polishing, oven cleaning, dishwashing, bathroom cleaning and window cleaning to the domestic market. They charged customers £10 per hour. They built up a strong customer base very quickly as they offered a high-quality personal service.

CURRENT SITUATION

The business expanded very quickly and they diversified into office and retail cleaning. They recruited two members of staff in order to help them meet the needs of these new clients.

Divya and Dev have started to receive complaints from clients. This has upset them, as one of their main aims was to offer a quality service. This poor service was the result of poor time management and lack of administration skills. Divya took responsibility for the bookings and

scheduling of clients, but she had to do this in between her cleaning jobs. Dev continued to clean for some of the domestic customers and also to transport his two workers to and from their jobs. He sometimes left jobs before the allotted time in order to do this and made one particular client so angry that she cancelled her contract. On the financial side Divya and Dev sometimes find that customers do not pay on time. They are concerned this may lead to future cash flow problems.

The partners realised that they could no longer operate from Divya's spare room. Accommodation is required to run the business successfully and implement procedures to ensure clients are fully satisfied.

OPTIONS FOR THE FUTURE

To eliminate the problems in the business and expand further, the partners have discussed the following options:

Option 1   Take on another partner.

Option 2   Set up a company website.

Option 3   Rent office premises.

Option 4   Hire an administrative assistant.

They have chosen options 2, 3 and 4.

QUESTIONS

Marks

1   From the options for the future, Clean4me chose options 2, 3 and 4.

   (a)   Give one reason to explain why they chose option 4.   **1**

   (b)   Give one advantage and one disadvantage of choosing option 2.   **2**

   (c)   Give 2 reasons why they did not choose option 1.   **2**

2   Other than a partnership, describe one **other** type of private sector business that Divya and Dev could have set up.   **1**

3   The school **outsourced** their cleaning.

   (a)   Define the term 'outsourcing'.   **1**

   (b)   Give 2 advantages of this to an organisation.   **2**

4   Clean4me is in the tertiary sector of industry.

   (a)   Identify and describe the 2 **other** sectors of industry.   **4**

(b) Give an example of an activity in each sector identified in (a).   **2**

5 Describe how Clean4me could use each of the following software   **6**
packages in their business:

- spreadsheet
- database
- word processing

6 Divya and Dev used all their redundancy money to buy a small van and
cleaning equipment.

Describe 2 other sources of finance and give a different disadvantage   **4**
of each source.

(25)

SuperJam

This section should take you approximately 45 minutes. Read the following information, then answer the questions which follow.

BACKGROUND

Fraser Doherty developed his entrepreneurial skills from a very young age. He sold meat for a local butcher door-to-door when he was just 12 years old. Fraser's success as a door-to-door salesman gave him a taste for business and at the age of 14 he asked his gran to teach him how to make jam. It wasn't long before Fraser was selling his jam regularly at church fairs  and community events. Fraser then asked for help from his friends and family to increase his production capacity and he found himself producing thousands of jars of jam from his parent's kitchen. Fraser sold these jars at farmers' markets and delicatessen shops across Edinburgh.

CURRENT SITUATION

Fraser's big break came when he discovered a gap in the market. With its unhealthy and old-fashioned image, sales of jam had been in decline for a number of years. Fraser recognised there was an opportunity for him to grab and he developed the healthier *SuperJam*. Armed with a sample jar, Fraser approached a Waitrose jam buyer who was very impressed by both Fraser's passion for his product and also his strong entrepreneurial skills. 'Fraser managed to take a product that's regarded as old-fashioned and completely re-invent it, giving it an up-to-date makeover.' Fraser, now 18 years old, has secured a deal with Waitrose to supply jam in 130 of their stores in the UK, as well as deals with Tesco, Morrison's and Asda. Fraser has moved his production from his parent's kitchen to a local factory in order to cope with the demand, and has created a website (www.superjam.co.uk) to provide information to the public.

Although Fraser has learned a lot about the world of business from his own experiences, he has decided to study for a degree in Business and Accountancy at the University of Strathclyde. Running his own business and studying for a degree is very demanding on Fraser's time, however, the University has been very supportive.

Fraser is very ambitious and does not want his business to remain still. He is already considering how he can expand and is considering developing new flavours and extending his product range into other products, such as adding his jams to yoghurts. Fraser also sees value in approaching other supermarket chains both here and internationally in order to promote his range further.

Fraser has received lots of publicity about his successes. He has made TV appearances and has had many newspaper articles written about him. Fraser won an Enterprising Young Brit Award and won the student category in the Biggart Baillie Innovation Award in 2007. For someone so young, where does Fraser go now?

OPTIONS FOR THE FUTURE

Option 1   Continue with his Business and Accountancy degree course.

Option 2   Expand the company's product range.

Option 3   Expand into the international market.

Fraser has chosen to implement all three options for the future.

Adapted from: *Strathclyde People* magazine 2007, University of Strathclyde and www.superjam.co.uk

QUESTIONS

Marks

1   Fraser Doherty is an entrepreneur. Describe the term 'entrepreneur' and explain the role of an entrepreneur.   **2**

2 Fraser has chosen to implement all 3 options for the future.   **3**
Explain why he may have chosen to implement each option. You should
provide a different reason for each option.

3 (a) It is important for all businesses to keep control of their finance.   **3**
Explain the purpose of drawing up a cash budget.

    (b) Describe 2 sources of cash flow problems.   **2**

4 Fraser's business is in the secondary sector.

    (a) Describe the term 'secondary sector'.   **1**

    (b) Identify and describe the 2 other sectors of business activity   **4**
that exist.

5 'Fraser recognised there was an opportunity for him to grab and he
developed the healthier *SuperJam*.'

Fraser used primary and secondary information to research this gap   **2**
in the market. Describe the terms 'primary information' and 'secondary
information'.

6 Fraser believed the jam industry was in the decline stage of the   **3**
product life cycle. Describe 3 other stages of the product life cycle.

7 SuperJam is being sold in supermarkets around the UK. Explain why   **1**
manufacturers often choose to sell their products to retailers.

8 Organisations are influenced by external factors. Fraser's business was   **4**
influenced by the social factor that people are more health conscious
nowadays. Identify and describe 2 other external factors that may
influence an organisation.

(25)

CASE STUDY 13

Fifi and Ally

This section should take you approximately 45 minutes. Read the following information, then answer the questions which follow.

BACKGROUND

Cousins Fiona Hamilton and Alison Fielding opened their first store – *Fifi and Ally* – in Princes Square, Glasgow, in 2005. Their store offers quirky fashion, gifts and food and has proved a real hit with customers. Fifi and Ally was named one of the world's 100 must-visit stores in 2007 and it has already attracted thousands of visitors.

Fiona's background is as a chartered surveyor. Alison was Art Director of the UK's largest independent record label, Beggars Group. Fiona and Alison decided to join together to form a business to realise one of their childhood dreams. They both contributed personal finance to fund the business and also gained support from the Bank of Scotland.

CURRENT SITUATION

The success of Fifi and Ally has been fantastic. Fiona and Alison won the Most Entrepreneurial Company title in 2007's Evening Times Business Awards and they have had articles written about them in many business magazines. The owners are about to open a second city branch in Wellington Street, Glasgow, and are also currently scouring London for the right premises to house their unique blend of food, fashion and gifts in England.

To help with this expansion, Fifi and Ally have considered expanding their management team. They have already brought on board Brian Johnston. Brian has 34 years' experience in the banking industry so he has a great knowledge of the world of finance. Fiona and Alison are also looking at restructuring the company because of their expansion plans. This means

the business may evolve from a flat structure to a tall structure. Fifi and Ally are also considering advertising for catering staff to help staff their expansion plans.

Fiona and Alison are dedicated to making sure they provide the best-quality service possible. They want customers to feel like they are eating amongst friends and always look for suppliers that will give them an exclusive choice of wine, food and designs. Alison was recently quoted as saying:

'As well as our innovative menus and fabulous inexpensive wines, we source and showcase small, hard to find brands producing beautiful quality pieces as well as fresh new design talent with the capacity to expand as we expand. We want the Fifi and Ally brand to be synonymous with great food and wine and beautiful, stylish, luxury goods produced in limited runs.'

OPTIONS FOR THE FUTURE

Option 1 Expand the management team.

Option 2 Advertise for additional staff.

Option 3 Restructure the business to become a tall structure.

Fiona and Alison have chosen options 1 and 2.

Adapted from: Marianne Taylor, 'Fifi and Ally set to open London Store', *Evening Times*, **6 July 2007; and www.fifi-and-ally.com**

QUESTIONS

Marks

1 Identify and describe the type of business organisation operated by Fifi and Ally.　2

2 (a) Fiona and Alison received support from the Bank of Scotland. Describe 2 types of support the Bank of Scotland may have been able to offer them.　2

(b) Businesses can receive support from a number of sources. Using the sources listed below, describe the support each of these may offer. You should describe a different type of support for each. **3**

- Other local businesses
- Prince's Trust
- Accountant

3 Fiona and Alison have chosen options 1 and 2.

(a) Explain why they may not have chosen option 3. **1**

(b) Explain why they may have chosen option 1. **1**

(c) Explain why they may have chosen option 2. **1**

4 As with most businesses, Fifi and Ally need to consider offering staff training.

(a) Identify and describe 3 types of training the business may consider. **6**

(b) Training is often described as financially costly for organisations. Describe 2 other costs of training. **2**

5 Quality is of prime importance for Fifi and Ally. Describe 3 quality systems that a business could use to ensure the quality of their product/service. **3**

6 Fifi and Ally will need to use ICT to aid communication when they expand. Identify and describe 2 types of ICT that would improve communication. **4**

(25)

Party Products

This section should take you approximately 45 minutes. Read the following information, then answer the questions which follow.

BACKGROUND

Clare Thom formed her business *Party Products* in 2006, after completing a college course in Business Management. She realised, when planning her twenty-first birthday party, that there was a gap in the market for party goods. This was because there was not a one-stop shop for all the things that she required for her party.

With a loan from her parents and a small start-up grant from the Prince's Youth Trust Clare set up her company specialising in party merchandise. Her aim is to provide good-quality party products at a reasonable price. Examples of her party merchandise are: balloons, banners, badges, party poppers, trumpets, streamers and party hats, as well as ranges of tableware for both children's parties and adult events. In addition to this, Clare specialises in organising and setting up balloon decorations for parties and corporate events. She has found that this service is particularly popular for weddings.

Clare managed to rent a small shop in a central location and her services have proved to be very popular. She employs a Saturday assistant to help her cope with the workload; Saturday is usually the busiest day. She also employs her sister on a casual basis when there are large functions to be organised.

Clare has not invested money in advertising her business. Most of her customers are recommended by word of mouth or come across the shop by chance. Once they have used the shop, however, they often become repeat customers because of the high-quality service that Clare offers.

CURRENT SITUATION

The shop is in a good location with ample parking but Clare's landlord is going to increase the rent by 20% when the lease is due to be renewed. Clare is concerned about how this will affect her future profitability and her ability to keep her prices competitive.

Recently a rival shop has opened up less than one mile away from Clare's shop. The competitor offers additional services such as party planning and cake baking, and also gives discounts on bulk orders.

If Clare wishes to continue to be successful she will need to seriously consider her options for the future.

OPTIONS FOR THE FUTURE

Option 1   Diversify into party planning.

Option 2   Move to larger premises in another area.

Option 3   Increase advertising and promotions in local area.

Option 4   Launch a website.

After a great deal of consideration Clare has decided to choose options 3 and 4.

QUESTIONS

Marks

1   Clare is a sole trader. Identify and describe one **other** type of business   **2**
organisation that she could have formed.

2   Clare chose options 3 and 4.

    (a) Give one advantage of choosing option 3.   **1**

    (b) Give one disadvantage of choosing option 4.   **1**

    (c) Give one reason why Clare may not have chosen option 2.   **1**

3 Clare's business environment changed owing to a rival business opening up near by.

Describe 3 **other** external factors that may affect Clare's business. **3**

4 Creating a website and selling online will alter Clare's channel of distribution. This is an example of altering the place element of the marketing mix.

Describe how Clare's business could alter the other three elements of the marketing mix (product, price and promotion) to give a competitive advantage. **6**

5 Clare aims to provide a quality service to her customers.

(a) Give 2 other aims that a sole trader may have. **2**

(b) Suggest 3 ways that Clare can achieve a quality service. **3**

6 (a) Choose any two of the following and explain how a small business might use them: **2**

- spreadsheet
- database
- email
- presentation software

(b) Describe 2 costs and 2 benefits of using ICT in business. **4**

(25)

The Farmhouse Restaurant

This section should take you approximately 45 minutes. Read the following information, then answer the questions which follow.

BACKGROUND

Mira and Marcus Mountjoy run a shop from their farm selling fresh fruit, vegetables and dairy products. The shop has proved very popular and they are making a good profit from it.

When a restaurant in the town centre came up for sale they decided to buy it. Mira and Marcus were able to obtain a bank loan to help with the new venture.

They were keen to use a lot of their own home-grown produce in the restaurant. As they were still running their farm and shop and looking after their three children, they did not have time to run the restaurant as well. They employed a manager, chef and four assistants to do this. The new restaurant was advertised in the local paper, and a feature was made of the organic food on offer. One of the farm workers delivers fresh vegetables and dairy produce to the restaurant twice weekly. The restaurant uses suppliers for other goods required.

There was a lot of interest in the restaurant and Mira and Marcus were delighted with the number of customers.

CURRENT SITUATION

During recent months the number of customers has fallen. Figures from the Profit and Loss Account show that the restaurant is running at a loss. This is a worry for Marcus and Mira because they are still in the process of paying back the loan to the bank.

On a recent visit to the restaurant Marcus was disappointed when he saw the food being offered. The menu contained very few options and those options on offer consisted of high-fat meals instead of wholesome healthy ones. On questioning some customers it was found that they were disappointed with the quality of the food and surprised at the lack of alcoholic drinks on offer.

When Marcus questioned the manager, the manager told him that the chef did not have time to cook organic food and preferred to cook food that was easy to make, such as chips and burgers. On inspecting the freezers Marcus found they contained large supplies of frozen vegetables and chips. The manager informed Marcus that the healthy options took a long time to cook and that the customers got tired waiting.

Mira has started to work in the restaurant to help the chef. This is not an ideal solution because she does not have the time to devote to this. She also resents being away from the farm and her children.

Mira thinks that they should sell the restaurant. However, Marcus is keen to make it a success. It has a good location and he feels it has a lot going for it. Mira and Marcus have the following options:

OPTIONS FOR THE FUTURE

Option 1   Sell the restaurant.

Option 2   Employ a well-qualified chef to help the present chef prepare healthy food choices.

Option 3   Offer alcoholic drinks.

Option 4   Advertise the restaurant featuring new menus and offer a discount, e.g. two meals for the price of one, for a limited period to attract customers.

Option 5   Visit the restaurant on a regular basis to ensure staff and customers are happy.

Mira and Marcus have chosen options 2, 3, 4 and 5.

QUESTIONS

Marks

1   Mira and Marcus were able to obtain a loan from the bank. Describe   **2**
    2 other ways they might have used to finance the purchase of the
    restaurant.

2   New staff will be recruited for the restaurant. Outline the recruitment   **4**
    process used by many organisations.

3   Option 4 is one of the options chosen. Describe 2 other ways Mira   **2**
    and Marcus could promote the restaurant.

4   Suppliers are used for other goods needed to run the restaurant.   **5**
    Describe features of a good supplier.

5   Describe the benefits to the business of providing quality food.   **4**

6   The Profit and Loss account shows that the restaurant is running at a   **4**
    loss. Name 2 other financial statements used in business and
    describe what they are used for.

7   The restaurant operates in the tertiary sector. Identify and describe   **4**
    2 other sectors of activity.

(25)

SECTION
TWO

Exam Style Questions

Exam Style Questions

1   Apple has launched a new iPhone. It will combine mobile-phone technology with music and video iPod as well as a camera.

   (a) (i)   Explain why Apple may have used this extension strategy. (A diagram could be used to illustrate your answer.)   **3**

        (ii)   Describe 3 **other** extension strategies that could be used.   **3**

   (b) Identify and describe 3 methods of finance that Apple may have used in order to fund the development of the new iPhone.   **6**

   (c) Shareholders, employees and the Government are examples of stakeholders.

        (i)   Describe the interest of each of these stakeholders.   **3**

        (ii)   Explain the influence that each one of the stakeholders may have on the organisation.   **3**

   (d) Quality is important to manufacturers. Outline the main features of Quality Management (formerly TQM).   **4**

   (e) Describe 3 factors that can affect the structure of an organisation.   **3**

                                                           (25)

2   Sarah owns a shop that sells baby clothes in Cumbernauld. She has decided to open another branch in Glasgow. This is known as internal growth.

   (a) (i)   Identify and describe 3 other methods of growth.   **6**

        (ii)   Explain 2 reasons why a business may choose to grow.   **2**

   (b) Sarah will need to employ more staff to run this second branch. Describe the recruitment and selection procedure she is likely to go through to ensure the best people are chosen for the jobs.   **6**

   (c) (i)   New staff require training. Identify the type of training on offer to new staff.   **1**

        (ii)   Explain 3 costs and 3 benefits to an organisation of training staff.   **6**

   (d) Describe 4 ways Sarah could market her new branch.   **4**

                                                           (25)

Marks

3 (a) Describe the stages of a product's life cycle. Use a diagram to illustrate your answer.   **6**

   (b) Suggest 3 ways a business could extend the life of a product.   **3**

   (c) (i) Distinguish between the following types of decisions: **6**

   - strategic

   - tactical

   - operational

   (ii) Give an example of each type of decision.   **3**

   (d) Businesses are not allowed to discriminate on the grounds of gender or race. Explain how this might affect a business.   **2**

   (e) (i) Explain why the control of stock is important to a business.   **2**

   (ii) Describe the following terms: **3**

   - maximum stock level

   - minimum stock level

   - re-order level

   (25)

4 (a) A business is affected by its external environment. Explain each of the following influences and describe how each can affect a business.   **6**

   - social influences

   - political influences

   - economic influences.

   (b) Businesses use various methods to pay their employees. Identify and describe 3 methods a business might use to pay employees.   **6**

   (c) Explain why businesses sell a range of products.   **2**

   (d) Identify and describe 3 pieces of legislation that businesses must comply with.   **6**

   (e) (i) Define the term 'branding'.   **1**

   (ii) Describe 2 advantages and 2 disadvantages of branded products for a business.   **4**

   (25)

5 Rangers and Celtic Football Clubs are Public Limited Companies.

   (a) (i) Compare a Public Limited Company to a sole trader. Your answer should look at ownership, control and finance.   **6**

Marks

    (ii)   One of the objectives of these football clubs is to make a profit. Describe 2 objectives of a charity.   **2**

(b) All businesses have to make decisions. Identify and describe 3 types of decisions that organisations make.   **6**

(c) Quality is of prime importance to all organisations. Identify and describe 4 quality systems that organisations may use to ensure they produce products of a good quality.   **8**

(d) Describe the following items that can be found on a Balance Sheet: **3**

- current assets
- current liabilities
- fixed assets

(25)

6 (a) There are two types of limited companies: Private Limited Companies and Public Limited Companies. Describe the features of each type.   **4**

(b) Jim Morton runs a catering business. He wishes to expand. Suggest 3 ways he could finance the expansion of his business.   **3**

(c) (i)   Describe the following sectors of industry: **3**

- primary
- secondary
- tertiary

    (ii)   Give an example of an activity that takes place in each sector.   **3**

(d) (i)   Outline the differences between a hierarchical (tall) organisation structure and a flat organisation structure.   **4**

    (ii)   Suggest an organisation that may operate under each structure.   **2**

(e) Describe each of the following quality systems: **6**

- Benchmarking
- Quality Management (formerly TQM)
- Quality Assurance

(25)

7 Bird flu is an example of an environmental factor that affects businesses.

(a) (i)   Identify 5 other external factors.   **5**

    (ii)   Describe the effects that external factors may have on businesses.   **5**

Marks

(b) In 2005 Asda was named best employer at the Scottish National Business Awards.

    (i)   Explain why good employee relations are important to Asda.   **4**

    (ii) Define each of the following and suggest how Asda would use each: **6**

- job description
- reference
- application form

(c) (i)   Explain the purpose of a contract of employment.   **1**

    (ii) Identify 4 pieces of information that would be contained in a contract of employment.   **4**

(25)

8 (a) Describe the marketing mix.   **4**

    (b) Explain the stages of the product life cycle. Use a diagram to support your answer.   **7**

    (c) A computer manufacturer is keen to introduce just-in-time (JIT) as a method of stock control. Explain the term JIT and describe 2 costs and 2 benefits of such a system.   **5**

    (d) (i)   Organisations produce financial statements to monitor their finances. Identify 3 users of such statements and explain their interest.   **6**

        (ii) Organisations may use their financial statements to undertake ratio analysis. Describe 3 disadvantages of undertaking ratio analysis.   **3**

(25)

9 (a) (i)   All employees must be issued with a contract of employment. Explain the benefits of this for: **2**

- an employee
- an employer

        (ii) Outline 3 conditions contained in a contract of employment.   **3**

    (b) (i)   Describe the difference between internal recruitment and external recruitment.   **2**

        (ii) Explain the advantages of internal recruitment and external recruitment.   **4**

    (c) (i)   Name the 4 elements of the marketing mix.   **4**

        (ii) Explain why **each** element is important.   **4**

Marks

(d) Identify 3 types of information and state when it would be appropriate to use each type. **6**

(25)

10 When forming a limited company you must complete a legal process.

(a) Identify and describe the 2 documents that would be sent to the Registrar of Companies. **4**

(b) (i) Identify and describe one other type of business organisation in the private sector. **2**

(ii) Give one advantage and one disadvantage of your chosen organisation. **2**

(c) Many large companies have an organisation chart.

(i) Explain the purpose of an organisation chart. **2**

(ii) Define the term 'functional grouping' and give an example of an organisation that arranges its business in that way. **2**

(iii) Give 2 advantages and 2 disadvantages of organising a business into functional departments. **4**

(d) Samsung aims to raise sales of flat-screen TVs by 80% in 2007 (*Metro* 9 January 2007). This should raise their profitability.

(i) Identify and describe 2 profitability ratios. **4**

(ii) Give 3 reasons why ratios should not be Samsung's only measure of success. **3**

(e) Distinguish between formal and informal structures. **2**

(25)

11 (a) (i) All organisations have stakeholders who are interested in the success of their business.

Identify 4 stakeholders of a school and describe their interest. **8**

(ii) Using the stakeholders identified in (a)(i), explain how each of these stakeholders can show their influence. **4**

(b) Introducing ICT can often help large organisations improve their communication systems. Describe 4 methods of ICT which can aid communication. **4**

(c) The introduction of ICT can have both a positive and negative impact on organisations. Other than improved communication, describe 3 benefits and 3 costs of introducing ICT into an organisation. **6**

(d) Describe the impact each of the following pieces of legislation may have on an organisation: **3**

Marks

● Race Relations Act (1976)

● National Minimum Wage Act (1998)

● Health and Safety at Work Act (1974)

(25)

12 (a) Explain the following finance terms: 3

   ● current assets

   ● long-term liabilities

   ● gross profit

(b) A business has a negative cash flow at the end of the month.

  (i) Explain what is meant by negative cash flow.   1

  (ii) Suggest steps the business could take to avoid this in the future.   3

(c) Describe the type of support the following could give to someone starting up a new business: 4

   ● bank manager

   ● lawyer

   ● Prince's Trust

   ● local businesses

(d) Large businesses such as the Royal Bank of Scotland (RBS) have many stakeholders.

Identify 3 stakeholders of RBS and state their interest in the business.   6

(e) Businesses use a variety of pricing strategies. Describe the following: 3

   ● penetration pricing

   ● skimming pricing

   ● promotional pricing.

(f) Suggest what is important to a business when choosing a supplier.   5

(25)

13 The Health and Safety at Work Act 1974 states the duties of the employee and employers.

(a) Identify 3 duties of an employer.   3

(b) Describe 3 costs and 3 benefits of training staff.   6

(c) Distinguish between labour intensive production and capital intensive production.   4

Marks

(d) Many businesses have growth as their aim.

    (i)   Identify and describe 4 different methods of growth.   **8**

    (ii)   Identify and describe 2 methods of ICT that would help improve communication within a large organisation.   **4**

    (25)

14 (a)   (i)   All organisations are influenced by external factors. Identify and describe 4 external factors that can influence an organisation.   **8**

    (ii)   Describe the impact each of the factors identified in (a)(i) may have on an organisation.   **4**

(b) An Italian restaurant is trying to source a new supplier. Describe 5 factors they might consider when choosing their new supplier.   **5**

(c) Describe the following systems and explain how they can influence the quality of a product: **4**

    ● Quality Circles

    ● Benchmarking

(d) Businesses often experience cash flow problems. Describe 4 measures that businesses can use to improve their cash flow.   **4**

    (25)

15 Decision making is an important part of a manager's job.

(a)   (i)   Describe the effects of poor decision making on an organisation.   **3**

    (ii)   Give 3 examples of strategic decisions that an organisation may make.   **3**

(b) Describe 5 types of information that a manager may use and give an advantage of each.   **10**

(c) Most large retailers have websites. Describe the costs and benefits of e-commerce to an organisation.   **5**

(d) Businesses must ensure that they protect personal details that they hold.

    Identify the piece of legislation that states this and outline some of the main points covered.   **4**

    (25)

16 (a) Describe 3 different ways a business could increase its net profit.   **3**

(b) Name the 2 Final Accounts that a business would draw up.   **2**

Marks

(c) In October 2006, the Employment Equality (Age) Regulations were introduced.

    (i) Explain the purpose of this new law.   **1**

    (ii) Identify and describe 3 **other** pieces of legislation designed to protect employees.   **6**

(d) Distinguish between a works council and a trade union.   **2**

(e) Describe the following types of employment: **6**

- full-time
- part-time
- flexi-time

(f) (i) Describe 3 ways an employer can ensure that employees gain job satisfaction.   **3**

    (ii) Explain why it is important to the employer that workers are satisfied.   **2**

    (25)

17 (a) Ricky owns a small art shop in Dundee, and a rival art shop has recently opened. Describe 3 promotions that Ricky can undertake to attract lost customers back.   **3**

(b) Ricky's competitor undertook much market research before opening her business. Identify and describe the 2 types of market research that she may have undertaken. Give an example of each type of research.   **6**

(c) (i) Describe each of the following types of information that are used in modern businesses: **5**

- oral
- written
- graphical
- quantitative
- qualitative

    (ii) Describe 5 features of good-quality information.   **5**

(d) (i) Describe 4 stages of a decision-making model.   **4**

    (ii) Explain 2 disadvantages of using a decision-making model to make decisions.   **2**

    (25)

Marks

18 (a) 'Brewery giant in talks to take over chain of fish restaurants' (*The Herald*, 21 July 2007).

    (i) Describe the method of growth described above.   **1**

    (ii) Identify and describe 2 other methods of growth.   **4**

  (b) Identify and describe 3 types of training that employers use.   **6**

  (c) Explain why information gathered by an organisation must be accurate and up to date.   **2**

  (d) (i) Describe the purpose of a Trading Profit and Loss Account.   **2**

    (ii) Identify 3 ratios used by organisations and explain what each would be used for.   **6**

  (e) Describe 4 pieces of computer software that could be used in a hospital. (Your answer should state what each piece does.)   **4**

                                                            (25)

19 (a) Describe the product life cycle using a diagram to illustrate your answer.   **4**

  (b) Coca-Cola teamed up with iTunes to give away free music downloads to European Coca-Cola drinkers.

    Describe other ways Coca-Cola could use the 4 Ps to extend the life of their product.   **4**

  (c) Walkers is a popular brand of crisps.

    Outline 4 benefits of branding to a company.   **4**

  (d) (i) Identify and describe the most suitable method of production for manufacturing crisps.   **2**

    (ii) Describe 2 other types of production and give an example of a product manufactured using each method.   **4**

  (e) Identify 3 channels of distribution used by manufacturers.   **3**

  (f) Outline the problems of overstocking and understocking.   **4**

                                                            (25)

20 (a) (i) Jason opened his own business making coffee and dining tables. He is keen to expand and has advertised for staff in his local job centre. Identify and describe 3 types of tests that Jason may use in the selection process to help ensure he gets the best candidate for the job.   **6**

    (ii) Jason is keen to ensure all employees in his organisation are well trained. Describe 4 costs and 4 benefits of training staff.   **8**

  (b) In Jason's Final Accounts he has listed his 'debtors', 'creditors' and 'working capital'. Explain each of these terms.   **3**

Marks

(c) (i) Organisations often make changes to their structure.   **2**
Describe the following terms:

● de-layering

● downsizing

(ii) Explain 3 reasons why organisations may choose to   **6**
de-layer and 3 reasons why they may choose to downsize.

(25)

21 (a) Name 2 items contained in each of the following: **6**

● job application form

● job description

● person specification.

(b) Describe 3 promotional methods used by supermarkets to   **3**
attract customers.

(c) (i) Explain 2 reasons why businesses conduct market   **2**
research.

(ii) Identify and describe 2 methods of field research used by   **4**
businesses.

(d) Describe 3 ways that businesses make use of the internet.   **3**

(e) Describe 2 activities that take place in each of the following   **4**
departments of an organisation:

● the finance department

● the human resources department.

(f) Explain 3 factors that would affect the choice of location for a   **3**
new business.

(25)

22 Fraser Docherty is the successful teenage entrepreneur responsible for
creating 100% sugar-free jam.

(a) Describe the role of the entrepreneur.   **4**

(b) (i) Define the following sources of finance: **4**

● mortgage

● grant

● bank loan

● debenture

(ii) Give a different advantage and disadvantage of each of the   **8**
above sources of finance.

(c) When employees are unhappy at work they may take industrial action.

    (i) Identify and describe 3 forms of industrial action.   **6**

    (ii) Suggest the impact that industrial action may have on an organisation.   **3**

                                                             (25)

23 Deborah runs a company producing bath oils. She has recently changed the production process to make it more capital intensive.

  (a) (i) Explain the following terms: **2**

       ● capital intensive production

       ● labour intensive production.

    (ii) Describe 3 advantages and 3 disadvantages of capital intensive production.   **6**

  (b) Describe the following quality measures that Deborah may implement: **4**

    ● Quality Control

    ● Quality Assurance

    ● Benchmarking

    ● Quality Circles

  (c) Deborah is currently a sole trader. Describe two advantages and two disadvantages of being a sole trader.   **4**

  (d) (i) Explain why employees may take industrial action.   **1**

    (ii) Identify and describe 4 types of industrial action.   **8**

                                                             (25)

24 (a) Identify and describe the 4 factors of production.   **8**

  (b) (i) Describe 3 sources of finance.   **3**

    (ii) Outline a different advantage and disadvantage of each method you have described.   **6**

  (c) Explain the following terms: **3**

    ● outsourcing

    ● span of control

    ● de-layering

  (d) Explain 2 ways a database could be used in the control of stock.   **2**

Marks

(e) Describe the following types of employment: **3**

- flexi-time

- part-time

- temporary

(25)

25 The global cosmetic company Avon has recently undergone some restructuring of their organisation to flatten the structure.

(a) (i) Describe the term 'flat structure'. **2**

    (ii) Describe the benefits to be gained from this type of restructuring. **5**

(b) Center Parcs won 'Best UK Holiday Provider' in the prestigious Tommy's Parent Friendly Awards 2007.

    (i) Describe the benefits to the company of winning this award. **2**

    (ii) Describe the benefit to the customer. **1**

    (iii) Identify 2 **other** quality standards. **2**

(c) One of the best-known Indian food manufacturers, Patak's, is looking at ways to expand globally.

    (i) Identify 3 **other** objectives that Patak's may have. **3**

    (ii) Identify and decribe 3 methods of growth. **6**

    (iii) Decribe how ICT can help a firm become global. **4**

(25)

26 (a) (i) Large organisations often like to centralise stock control activities. Describe 2 advantages and 2 disadvantages of centralised stock storage. **4**

    (ii) Define the following stock control terms: **4**

- maximum stock level

- minimum stock level

- re-order level

- re-order quantity.

    (iii) Explain 2 difficulties of overstocking and 2 difficulties of understocking. **4**

(b) Describe the purpose of the following ratios: **3**

- gross profit percentage

- return on capital employed

- current ratio/working capital ratio

Marks

(c) Other than finance, describe 2 internal factors that can affect a business's performance.   **2**

(d) Identify and describe 4 external factors that can influence a business.   **8**

(25)

27 Ratios can help managers make decisions.

  (a) (i) Give 3 other uses of ratio analysis.   **3**

      (ii) Identify and describe the 3 financial areas of a business that ratios could be calculated for.   **6**

     (iii) Describe 2 limitations of using ratios.   **2**

  (b) Managers are also responsible for motivating employees.

      (i) Suggest 5 methods that a manager may use to increase staff motivation.   **5**

      (ii) Describe the possible effects of poorly motivated staff.   **3**

  (c) Distinguish between the following human resources terms: **6**

- full-time and part-time employment
- blue collar and white collar workers
- senior managers and junior managers.

(25)

28 The finance department is responsible for paying wages.

  (a) (i) Name the 2 main deductions taken from employee wages.   **2**

      (ii) Identify 2 **other** tasks that the finance department would be responsible for.   **2**

     (iii) Identify 3 **other** functional areas and describe a task each is responsible for.   **6**

  (b) Some organisations arrange their employees into teams.

     Describe the benefits of team working.   **4**

  (c) It was reported that some Standard Life customers could be at risk of fraud after their personal details were lost by HM Revenue & Customs (HMRC). (BBC News 3 November 2007)

      (i) Suggest how a company could protect personal data.   **3**

      (ii) Name the Act that exists to protect personal data   **1**

     (iii) Outline three drawbacks of using ICT (other than loss of data).   **3**

Marks

(d) Define the following operations terms: **4**

- lead time

- economies of scale

- inventory

- automation

(25)

29 Steven and Fraser are keen to start a business selling package holidays.

(a) (i) Identify and describe 2 methods of market research they   **6**
may undertake. Give an example of a type of market research
for each method identified.

(ii) Since Steven and Fraser will be unable to conduct market   **4**
research on the entire population, identify and describe 2
methods of sampling they may use.

(b) Explain 4 pricing strategies that Steven and Fraser may   **4**
consider when opening their business.

(c) Identify and describe 4 pieces of legislation that Steven and   **8**
Fraser would need to abide by when recruiting staff for their new
business.

(d) Managing employee relations can be a difficult task for any manager.   **3**
Explain the purpose of the following employee relation terms:

- trade unions

- industrial action

- ACAS (Advisory, Conciliation and Arbitration Service)

(25)

30 (a) Explain the difference between random sampling and quota sampling.   **2**

(b) Outline the benefits of staff training for both employees and   **4**
organisations.

(c) Molly Miller is a sole trader who is thinking of taking a partner
into her business.

(i) Describe 2 advantages and 2 disadvantages of   **4**
partnership.

(ii) Explain the role of an entrepreneur.   **2**

(d) Explain the following terms: **3**

- input

- process

- output

Marks

(e) Describe the following pricing strategies: **3**

- competitive pricing

- loss leaders

- price discrimination

(f) (i) Describe actions that employees may take if they are **4**
threatened with job cuts.

(ii) Describe the term 'corporate culture' and explain 2 ways **3**
that an organisation's culture may be evident.

(25)

31 (a) Distinguish between the following types of business organisations. **9**

- sole trader

- Partnership

- Public Limited Company

(b) Suggest possible objectives that an organisation in the voluntary **4**
sector may have.

(c) (i) Describe how ICT could help with the following tasks: **3**

- maintenance of records

- marketing a new product

- provision of information.

(ii) Describe the possible effect on employees of the introduction **3**
of new ICT.

(d) Decisions that owners of a business make may affect their cash flow.

(i) Suggest 3 methods that a business may use to avoid cash **3**
flow problems.

(ii) Describe 3 limitations of ratio analysis. **3**

(25)

32 Mairi and Karen have opened a business making fashionable clothes
for people aged 15–30 years old.

(a) (i) Identify and describe 3 types of production methods they **6**
may use.

(ii) Explain one advantage and one disadvantage of each type of **6**
production method identified in part (a)(i). A different
advantage and disadvantage should be used for each
production method.

(b) Describe 4 'into the pipeline' promotions that Mairi and Karen **4**
may use.

Marks

(c) (i) Explain what is meant by the term 'span of control'. 1

(ii) Distinguish between a narrow span of control and a wide span of control. 2

(d) Mairi and Karen will have to make strategic, tactical and operational decisions in their business. Describe strategic, tactical and operational decisions and give an example of each type of decision in relation to Mairi and Karen's business. 6

(25)

33 (a) Name 3 stakeholders of the National Health Service and explain how each can show their influence. 6

(b) Describe the differences between labour intensive production and capital intensive production. 2

(c) Managers are responsible for making important decisions. 5

(i) Describe a decision-making model they may use.

(ii) Outline 4 factors that might affect the quality of a decision. 4

(d) Name 2 items which are contained in each of the following financial documents:

(i) Trading Profit and Loss Account. 2

(ii) Balance Sheet. 2

(e) (i) Outline the differences between a tall organisation structure and a flat organisation structure. 2

(ii) Give an example of an organisation that operates under each structure. 2

(25)

34 (a) The finance department is responsible for maintaining financial records.

Explain the purpose of producing financial records. 4

(b) Shell is an example of a multinational company.

(i) Explain why a company might become a multinational. 4

(ii) Identify 3 disadvantages that multinationals may bring to their host country. 3

(c) (i) Identify 3 pieces of ICT that would help a multinational company communicate with all its branches. 3

(ii) Suggest how the multinational may use each piece of ICT identified. 3

Marks

(d) The operations department is dependent on other departments in the organisation if it is to run smoothly.

Explain how the following departments may assist the operations department:

6

● marketing

● finance

● human resources

(e) Describe the features of a strategic decision.

2

(25)

35 (a) All organisations have a number of stakeholders who are interested in their success. Describe the interest of each of the stakeholders listed below and explain how they show their interest:

10

● owner

● employee

● customer

● suppliers

● Government

(b) Identify and describe 4 types of information organisations may use.

8

(c) (i) Explain what is meant by the term 'out of the pipeline' promotions.

1

(ii) Describe 4 'out of the pipeline' promotions that a restaurant may use.

4

(d) Describe 2 methods of on-the-job training.

2

(25)

36 (a) (i) Identify 3 ways that customers can be divided into different market segments.

3

(ii) Market researchers often use questionnaires to obtain meaningful information. Describe 4 characteristics of a good questionnaire.

4

(b) Explain 2 disadvantages of overstocking.

2

(c) Describe the characteristics of the following types of business organisation:

6

● sole trader

● partnership

● Private Limited Company

Marks

(d) Describe the following types of information and explain when it would be suitable to use each of them:

- graphical
- oral
- pictorial
- written

8

(e) Outline the duties of both the employer and employee in respect of the Health and Safety at Work Act.

2

(25)

37 (a) (i) Describe the importance of market research to an organisation.

4

(ii) Identify possible problems that may be associated with market research.

5

(b) Internet campaigners influenced Cadbury to relaunch the Wispa chocolate bar.

Identify and describe the influence of 4 **other** stakeholders in Cadbury.

8

(c) Identify and describe 4 sources of information that Cadbury may use to make decisions.

8

(25)

38 (a) Describe the following types of business organisation:

- Public Limited Company
- Private Limited Company

4

(b) All organisations have objectives. Describe 4 objectives that organisations may work towards achieving.

4

(c) Explain the line relationships and functional relationships that exist in organisations.

2

(d) (i) Explain 3 factors that could influence an organisation's choice of advertising.

3

(ii) Describe one advantage and one disadvantage of the following types of field research. You should use a different advantage and disadvantage for each type of field research.

8

- telephone survey
- postal survey
- hall test
- personal interview

EXAM STYLE QUESTIONS

Marks

(e) Identify and describe 2 payment systems that organisations often use.   **4**

(25)

39 (a) Explain the following terms: **3**

- trade credit

- mortgage

- retained profit

(b) Explain the term 'external information' and give 3 examples.   **4**

(c) Organisations often use promotion to encourage sales.

    (i)   Explain the difference between 'into the pipeline' promotion and 'out of the pipeline' promotion.   **2**

   (iii)   Describe 2 'into the pipeline' promotions and 2 'out of the pipeline' promotions used by organisations.   **4**

(d) Explain why the following are interested in an organisation's financial information: **5**

- managers

- potential investors

- banks

- Inland Revenue

- suppliers

(e) Organisations use various methods when training staff. Describe each of the following methods: **3**

- coaching

- job rotation

- distance learning

(f) Outline the selection process used by organisations to find the right person for a job.   **4**

(25)

40 (a) Competition is one external factor that has an affect on an organisation. Identify 4 other external factors and explain the effects each may have on an organisation.   **8**

(b) Explain 3 methods that organisations could use to extend the life of a product.   **3**

(c) Outline 4 reasons why organisations carry out staff appraisals.   **4**

Marks

(d) Describe one advantage and one disadvantage of each of the
following types of information: **6**

- primary

- secondary

- internal

(e) Outline 2 objectives of a public sector organisation and 2 different
objectives of a charity.   **4**

(25)

41 (a) Erin opened a gym in Falkirk. The business was very successful,
but recently Erin has been experiencing cash flow problems.
Identify 3 sources of cash flow problems and explain how a
business could resolve each of these problems.   **6**

(b) Erin is not the only person interested in the gym's financial
information. Explain the interest the following people have in the
gym's financial information: **4**

- employees

- suppliers

- bank

- local community

(c) (i) Erin is considering introducing ICT into her business.
Describe 2 advantages and two disadvantages of this for
both Erin and her employees.   **8**

    (ii) Identify a piece of software that would allow Erin to calculate
her finances.   **1**

(d) (i) Explain the 3 channels of distribution available to
organisations.   **3**

    (ii) Describe 3 factors that could influence the channel of
distribution that a business chooses.   **3**

(25)

42 (a) Explain 3 reasons why organisations use cash budgets.   **3**

(b) (i) Identify and describe 3 different quality methods used by
organisations to ensure high-quality products are produced.   **6**

    (ii) Products are produced using different methods of production.
Name 3 methods used to produce goods.   **3**

    (iii) Give an example of a product made by each method identified
in (b) (ii).   **3**

Marks

(c) (i) Outline the differences between a centralised organisation structure and a decentralised organisation structure. **2**

(ii) Describe one advantage and one disadvantage of each type of structure. **4**

(d) Describe 2 costs and 2 benefits of using the internet for an organisation. **4**

(25)

43 (a) (i) Identify 3 methods of advertising. **3**

(ii) Describe 3 possible factors that would affect the choice of advertising used. **3**

(b) When choosing a method of advertising, a manager may use a structured decision-making model. **5**

Outline the stages of a structured decision-making model.

(c) Stock is an expensive item, which should be stored properly to avoid damage. **5**

Describe the qualities of a good stock room.

(d) (i) Define the term 'hierarchical structure'. **1**

(ii) Suggest 2 costs and 2 benefits associated with this type of organisational structure. **4**

(iii) Identify and describe 2 other types of organisational structure. **4**

(25)

44 (a) (i) Marcus is keen to begin his own business as a soft drink manufacturer. Identify and describe 3 methods of field research he may use to gather information from his potential market. **6**

(ii) Explain one advantage and one disadvantage of each method of field research identified in part (a)(i). You should use a different advantage and disadvantage for each method of field research. **6**

(b) If Marcus were to take on employees to help him in the business, identify and describe 4 payment systems he may use. **8**

(c) (i) Marcus is trying to decide whether his business would be a labour intensive or capital intensive production process. Explain one factor that may influence his choice. **1**

(ii) Describe one advantage and one disadvantage of both labour intensive production and capital intensive production. You should use a different advantage and disadvantage for each method of production. **4**

(25)

Marks

45 (a)   (i)   Just-in-time stock control is used by many organisations.

            Explain just-in-time stock control.   **1**

      (ii)   Describe 2 advantages and 2 disadvantages of this   **4**
method of stock control.

   (b)   (i)   Jade Stevens hopes to open up a hairdressing business.   **3**
Describe 3 factors she should take into account when
deciding how much to charge customers.

      (ii)   Describe 2 ways Jade could promote her business.   **2**

   (c)   Explain the difference between desk research and field research.   **2**

   (d)   Describe 3 types of tests that applicants applying for jobs may   **3**
have to undergo.

   (e)   Name 3 functional departments of an organisation and   **6**
describe an activity that takes place in each.

   (f)   Information plays a vital part in all organisations. Identify 4   **4**
characteristics of good information.

                                                                        (25)

Solutions – Case Study Questions

Marks

Case study 1 Garlic

1 *(a)* • Analyse application forms/CVs

4

           • Invite suitable candidates for tests

           • Invite suitable candidates for interviews/carry out interviews

           • Offer the most suitable candidate the job

           • Inform unsuccessful candidates

    (b) Induction training – training that is given to new employees to make them familiar with the business and their job

2

2 *(a)* • To gain more profits

3

           • To gain a bigger market share

           • To become more well-known

           • To avoid becoming the target for a takeover

           • To reduce the risk of the business failing

           • To reduce or eliminate competitors

           • To take advantages of economies of scale

    (b) • Horizontal integration – where firms producing the same products/services combine together

3

           • Forward vertical integration – where a firm takes over a customer – e.g. a farmer takes over a butcher shop

           • Backward vertical integration – where a firm takes over a supplier – e.g. a petrol station taking over an oil refinery

           • Conglomerate integration (diversification) – where a firm takes over a business that operates in a completely different market

           • Internal growth – where a company decides to expand itself – e.g. by opening another store

3 *(a)* • To open up the business to the world-wide market

1

           • To increase sales/profits

    (b) • To stay ahead of competitors

1

           • To have a unique selling point

           • To cash in on the trend to learn how to cook

    (c) • The Eusebi family already offer a healthy eating range as part of their product range.

1

           • Only supplying healthy food would narrow down the market

4 • Functional groupings – organised into departments where people have similar skills and expertise, e.g. marketing, human resources, finance

4

    • Product/service grouping – where the organisation is grouped around its product/service and each department deals with a different product

- Customer grouping – where the organisation is grouped around different types of customers
- Place/territory grouping – where the organisation is grouped according to the different geographical areas
- Technology grouping – where an organisation groups its activity according to the technological or production processes

5 (a) • Word processing packages –software used to create and manipulate text   2
- Database packages – software used for keeping records – e.g. staff, customers
- Spreadsheet packages – software used to carry out calculations
- Desktop publishing packages – software used to produce quality documents with text and graphics
- Computer Aided Design packages – software used to create 3-D designs
- Email – communication can take place instantly from one computer to another. Information can reach people across the world very quickly, regardless of time differences
- Video-conferencing – allows people to see one another despite being in different locations around the world. Allows people to see each other's reactions, but does not involve the cost of flights or accommodation to facilitate this
- Mobile telephone – people can be contacted almost anywhere to discuss issues
- Networks – people can share information on a local area network (LAN) or wide area network (WAN)
- Laptops – portable computer

(b) Benefits   4
- Increased productivity
- Less error/wastage
- More consistent quality
- Cheaper than employing more staff
- Can operate 24 hours, seven days per week – without breaks

Costs
- Costly to train staff
- If machinery breaks down, production can stop
- Staff can feel de-motivated
- Viruses can corrupt data

(25)

Case study 2 Star Sparkles

1 • Innovative product – benefit of this is there is little or no competition   4
- Lots of demand – benefit of this is that Pauline can make much profit from the business
- Lots of interest from other companies – benefit of this is that this may help Pauline gain more profit and expand her business

2 (a) • This is a business owned and controlled by one person. This person organises the finance for the business and takes all the profit   1

(b) • Partnership – a business owned by 2–20 people   4
- Private Limited Company – a business that sells shares to friends/family
- Public Limited Company – a business that sells shares on the stock exchange

Marks

3 *(a)* These stores could bring Pauline lots of business and therefore increased profits   1

    (b) • Pauline currently gets much business via her website so she would want this to continue   1

       • The website allows people worldwide to purchase her product 24 hours a day, seven days a week

    (c) It would be expensive to set up her own shop and employ additional staff   1

4 • People worldwide can see what the business has to offer   2

    • The business can use the website to gather information from customers

    • The business can use the website to advertise new offers

    • The business can use the website to advertise new products

5 • Internal recruitment – advertise the job within the organisation (e.g. via noticeboards, newsletters)   2

    • External recruitment – advertise the job outside the organisation (e.g. via newspaper, job centre)

6 *(a)* Product endorsement/sponsorship   1

    (b) • Fans of Paris Hilton will want to buy the product too   1

       • The product will become more well-known

7 • Introduction – product is introduced into the market, sales are low and little or no profit is being made. No competition for this product   5

    • Maturity – sales and profits reach their peak. Competition starts to emerge

    • Decline – sales and profits are reduced. Product/service may be removed from the market. Market is saturated with competitors

    • Diagram – 3 marks available – 1 mark for appropriate labelling of axis, 1 mark for appropriate curve, 1 mark for appropriate labelling of stages

8 • Operations – department that makes the product and checks it for quality   2

    • Finance – department that draws up the Final Accounts, pays employees' wages, issues invoices to customers, pays suppliers

                  (25)

Case study 3 Growing Pains

1 • Could be done fairly easily and the cost would be reasonable   2

    • Option 1 would allow for 20 tables and chairs whereas option 2 would only allow for 9 tables and chairs

    • If option 2 had been chosen, less space would have been available for displaying goods and this might have resulted in reduced sales

2 • Good quality products   4

    • Products delivered on time

    • Acceptable price

    • Discounts

    • Is the supplier able to supply quantity required?

    • Does supplier have a good reputation?

3 • Prepare a job analysis   **4**
  • Prepare a job description
  • Prepare a person specification
  • Advertise the job

4 Advantages   **4**
  • Workload can be shared
  • More finance available
  • Partners can bring different skills to the business
  • Partnership is in a stronger position to apply for finance than a sole trader

  Disadvantages
  • Partners have unlimited liability
  • Profits have to be shared
  • Partners may disagree
  • If partner dies or leaves, a new partnership agreement must be set up

5 *(a)* • Grant does not usually have to be paid back   **2**
  • Loan does have to be paid back and interest is charged

  (b) • Government   **2**
  • Local authority
  • Enterprise agencies
  • Prince's Trust

6 • Offer a range of Xmas gifts and decorations for sale   **2**
  • Special offers – buy one, get one free
  • Have a Santa's Grotto for children where they receive gifts
  • Advertise the tearoom offering attractive meals

7 • Advertise it in the newspapers, local radio, television, internet, etc.   **3**
  • Send out mailshots

8 • Employer must ensure that premises are safe for employees to work in   **2**
  • Employees must behave in a suitable manner so as not to cause any unnecessary health hazard to other employees

Case study 4 Cuppa Chino

1 • Well researched   **2**
  • She had the initial start-up capital
  • Knew the local area well
  • Had a USP, soft-play area
  • Gained advice from Small Business Gateway

2 *(a)* • To remind customers she exists   **1**
  • To persuade customers to visit her shop
  • To attract new customers
  • To inform customers of the new services

Marks

(b) • Introduce a loyalty card – encourage customers to return   **4**
   • Buy one get one free – to encourage customers to buy more products
   • Discounts – to entice customers away from competitors

(c) • Decision making would be harder   **2**
   • She would have to share the profits

3 • A lease is a method of renting; the property/equipment will never belong to you   **2**
   • A mortgage is a long-term loan secured on a property; once the mortgage has been repaid you will own the property

4

Stakeholders:	Customers	Environmental Health	Employees	
Influence	may go to competitors	may close business down	poor service	**3**
Impact	may have to offer cheaper prices	may have to implement strict cleanliness rules	may have to provide training/appraisals	**3**

5 (a) • Trading Profit and Loss Account – both the gross profit and net profit would fall   **2**
   • Balance Sheet – the net worth figure would fall

(b) • To calculate the amount of money coming in and going out   **2**
   • To calculate if there is enough cash to buy new equipment/expand
   • To calculate if you can pay bills
   • To forecast when you might require additional finance

6 (a) • Field research – the collection of primary information   **2**
   • Desk research – the collection and use of secondary information

(b) • Field research examples – surveys, postal questionnaires, interviews   **2**
   • Desk research examples – internet, books and newspapers

(25)

Case study 5 IKEA

1 (a) • Flat Structure – an organisation with few levels of management. There is a short chain of command which means that departments have more independence. Information can be easily and quickly passed between departments. This structure is suitable for small to medium sized organisations   **2**
   • Tall Structure – an organisation with many levels of management. Decisions and information are passed down from senior management. Communication tends to be slow as it has many levels to pass through. This structure is suitable for large organisations

(b) **Wide span of control**: When a manager has many subordinates under his control.   **1**

2 • Personal interview – this involves face-to-face interview asking questions and receiving instant responses   **6**
   • Postal survey – this involves sending out questionnaires through post or email asking people to return them
   • Telephone survey – this involves telephoning people at home and asking questions

Marks

3   Recruitment Process   **6**
  - Identify Job Vacancy
  - Conduct Job Analysis
  - Prepare Job Description
  - Prepare Person Specification
  - Advertise job
  - Send out Application Forms

    Selection Process
  - Check applications against Person Specification
  - Draw up short list
  - Carry out relevant tests
  - Hold interviews
  - Check references
  - Decide on best candidate
  - Offer position
  - Once accepted, inform unsuccessful candidates

4   - Stores such as Asda, Tesco and Marks & Spencer now offer a wide range of home   **4**
      furnishings, etc. which make it convenient for customers to buy these goods while doing
      their normal shopping
    - Ikea stores are situated in retail parks and require customers travelling to them

5   - To remain competitive   **3**
    - To offer a wide range of home furnishes
    - To offer well designed goods at low prices

6   - Government – could increase taxation which results in further expenditure for Ikea.   **3**
      Introduce laws that Ikea must comply with
    - Customers – if they are dissatisfied with the service offered at Ikea they can take their
      custom elsewhere
    - Suppliers – they can increase their prices; refuse to give discounts; demand immediate
      payment for goods supplied

                                                                                   (25)

Case study 6 Scottish Signs

1   *(a)* A legal document that helps to set out the conditions of the partnership and avoid any   **1**
           disputes

    (b) - How profits and losses will be shared   **2**
           - Responsibilities of each partner
           - How much salary each will get paid

2   *(a)* - John and Jenny will still receive profits   **1**
           - The employee is experienced and knows the business well
           - Customers will receive continuity

    (b) - They will still have the worry of owning the business   **1**
           - The employee has no management experience

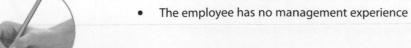

Marks

(c) • High cost of salary   **1**

     • High cost of recruitment of professional manager

     • May not please loyal customers

     • May not please the current staff

3 • Diversification – when you introduce new products or buy over a firm in a completely different market   **3**

   • Organic – when a company grows through increasing their sales and/or staffing

   • Vertical integration – when a company joins with another in the same industry but at a different stage of production

4 Advantages

   • Production quality will be consistent   **4**

   • Reduction in waste

   • Machines do not require breaks/holidays etc.

   Disadvantages

   • High initial cost of buying equipment

   • Staff training

   • Production may stop if equipment breaks down

5 (a) • They could take industrial action   **2**

     • The standard of their work will affect the quality/reputation of business

   (b) • Owners – high profits   **4**

     • Banks – in the ability to meet loan repayments

     • Customers – high quality at a reasonable price

     • Community – in the provision of jobs

     • Government – that the company is complying with legislation

6 (a) (i) Off the job   **1**

     (ii) On the job – training that takes place within the organisation whilst carrying out the job   **1**

   (b) Costs

     • The cost of the training course itself   **4**

     • Loss of efficiency until staff are trained

     • Cost of cover staff

     • Loss of output while training

     Benefits

     • Staff are more efficient

     • Fewer errors/accidents/wastage

     • Greater output

     • Increase in staff motivation and morale

(25)

Case study 7 Healthy Options

1 (a) Franchise: a business agreement that allows a business to use the name of another business and sell that business's products   **1**

Marks

(b) Advantages
- No need to advertise as business is usually advertised on a national scale
- Risk of failure is reduced as business usually well established and well known

2

Disadvantages
- Franchiser may dictate certain rules and conditions which franchisee must comply with
- A percentage of all profits goes to the franchiser

2

2 (a)
- They could have asked the bank for a loan
- They could have applied to the Government, local authority or enterprise trust for a grant

(b) Bank loan – advantage
- Can be repaid over a set period of time
- Fairly easy to obtain

4

Bank loan – disadvantage
- Interest is charged on the loan

Grant – advantage
- Does not usually have to be repaid

Grant – disadvantage
- Certain restrictions may apply to the grant, e.g. to give work to long-term unemployed

3
- Identify any problems that may exist
- Identify the objectives of the decision
- Identify any constraints
- Gather information which may help your decision
- Analyse the information gathered
- Devise possible solutions
- Select the best solution
- Communicate the decision to those concerned
- Plan and implement the decision
- Evaluate the effectiveness of the decision made

5

4
- Offer discounts and promotions to encourage cash sales and reduce high stock levels
- Sell any fixed assets no longer required
- Arrange credit terms with suppliers
- Reduce owner's drawings
- Try to introduce more finance into business, e.g. a partner

4

5
- Identify job vacancy
- Conduct job analysis
- Prepare job description
- Prepare person specification
- Advertise job vacancy
- Send out application forms

4

6
- Political factors: Government may introduce new laws that business must comply with
- Economic factors: rise in interest rates would mean increased expense for business
- Competitive factors: other business may sell similar products at reduced price

3

Marks

Case study 8 Perfect Paws

1
- Option 1 – Does not want to lose her present clients
- Option 2 – Would allow her business to expand
- Option 3 – She requires help to run and expand her business

3

2
- Partnership: a business with 2–20 partners who own and control the business. Unlimited liability; profits have to be shared among partners
- Private Limited Company: shares are owned privately. Has a minimum of one shareholder. Owned by shareholders and run by a director or Board of Directors
- Public Limited Company: shares are available for the public to purchase. Must have a minimum of two shareholders and £50,000 share capital. Board of Directors control it
- Franchise: business that uses another business's name and sells their products/services. Franchiser (company that owns business) receives a percentage of profits

6

3
- Temporary: employed as and when needed
- Part-time: employed for only part of working week, e.g. morning/afternoons or set number of hours
- Full-time: employed for full working week

3

4
- He will receive money for rent of room.
- He may also gain customers from Nicola's business

2

5 Family and friends
- Disadvantage: may wish to be paid back sooner rather than later
- Can lead to disagreements

Loan from bank
- Disadvantage: interest is charged on loan
- If interest rates are high this can prove very expensive

Venture capital
- Disadvantage: often charge a large fee
- May insist on part ownership of business

4

6 Health and Safety at Work Act 1974
- Employers must provide a safe place of work for employees

Sex Discrimination Act 1975
- Men and women must be treated equally and fairly in the workplace

Race Relations Act 1976
- No discrimination should be made because of an employee's race, colour, nationality or ethnic origin

Disability Discrimination Act 1995
- It is unlawful to discriminate against disabled employees. Employees must make adjustments in the workplace to accommodate disabled employees

National Minimum Wage Regulations 1999
- This sets out the minimum wage that must be paid to employees

4

7
- Internet: would allow Nicola to advertise her business and also buy any goods she may require to run her business
- Database: would allow Nicola to store names, addresses, etc. of customers

3

- Spreadsheet: would allow Nicola to calculate employees' wages and keep financial records
- Word processing: would allow Nicola to create documents such as letters, memos, etc.
- Email: would allow Nicola to send and receive mail instantly

Case study 9 Soft and Pure Skin Solutions

1 (a) Becoming a Public Limited Company means the company will sell shares to the public on the stock market   1

   (b) • A PLC requires a minimum start-up capital of £50,000   2
        • A PLC can sell on the stock exchange whereas a limited company must invite people to invest privately in the business

2 (a) • Carry out market research   2
        • Begin a marketing campaign
        • Find public relation possibilities
        • Raise the profile of company
        • Introduce promotions
        • Find ways of extending the life cycle of products

   (b) • Shortlist candidates by looking at CVs and application forms   5
        • Invite candidates for interviews
        • Involve candidates in testing, e.g. psychological etc
        • Take up candidates references
        • Ask candidates to give presentations
        • Select the most suitable candidate

3 • It would lose some control of business
   • Conflicts might arise between franchiser and franchisee
   • Monitoring of standards might be difficult
   • The franchisee might do something that would jeopardise the brand

4 (a) • Will extend product range and spread risk   1
        • Will increase profits as targeting a wider market
        • Will extend the product life cycle
        • Will increase profits

   (b) • It can tailor the advertisements to the correct people   2
        • Changes can be made more easily to products if you are aware of who you are selling to
        • The pricing can be set at the correct level for the people who are buying the products

5 (a) Batch production: groups of similar products can be made in sets and then machinery changed to produce a different type of product   2

   (b) (i) Job or flow production   1

        (ii) Job production – advantages   4
             • Product can be made to customer specifications
             • High product quality
             • Workers are motivated

Job production – disadvantages
- High labour costs
- Time taken to make product
- May not be suitable for all types of products

Flow production – advantages
- Can produce vast quantities of products
- Products can be standardised – consistent quality
- Benefit from economies of scale

Flow production – disadvantages
- High costs for machinery
- All products are identical
- Workers may lack motivation due to repetitive nature of job

6 *(a)*
- Looking for ways to enhance existing products
- Developing new products

2

(b)
- Gives the company a unique selling point (USP)
- Can create positive publicity
- Will encourage people to buy from the company
- Increase in sales and profits

1

(25)

Case study 10 Ollie Clothing

1
- Product becomes instantly recognisable
- Customers trust the product and see it as good quality
- Brand loyalty often develops
- Can allow the business to launch new products with little advertising

3

2 *(a)* Option 1
- Could lead to a huge increase in profits
- Could lead to a huge increase in market share
- Company would become more well-known
- May benefit from economies of scale (growth advantages)

3

Option 2
- Could compete more effectively with competitors
- Reach another market so profits should increase

Option 3
- Consumers could buy online leading to increased profits
- Customers world-wide could access the company

(b)
- Horizontal integration – where firms producing the same products/services combine together
- Forward vertical integration – where a firm takes over a customer, e.g. a farmer takes over a butcher shop
- Backward vertical integration – where a firm takes over a supplier, e.g. a petrol station taking over an oil refinery
- Conglomerate integration (diversification) – where a firm takes over a business that operates in a completely different market
- Internal growth – where a company decides to expand itself, e.g. by opening another store

6

(c) • Bank loan – where banks give people a specific sum of money which must be repaid with interest
      4

• Grant – money given to an organisation e.g. by the Government, Prince's Trust or National Lottery which does not need to be paid back

• Leasing – where a business rents pieces of equipment instead of tying up money by buying the equipment outright

• Hire purchase – where a business pays a deposit for a piece of equipment and then pays the rest in regular instalments

• Venture capital – money that is loaned to a business by a venture capitalist where a bank may have considered the venture too risky

3 (a) • Advertising – on TV, radio, magazines, fliers
      4

• Credit facilities – offer consumers the opportunity to buy on credit if they purchase online

• Competition – offer consumers the opportunity to win – e.g. vouchers – if they purchase online

• Buy one, get one free offers

• Free delivery – items will be delivered for nothing if consumers purchase online

(b) • Human resource costs – lower for the website as the company would not need to employ staff to sell products in the shop
      2

• Running expenses – lower for the website as the company would not need to have a shop from which to sell the product/service and would not need to pay for electricity, heating, lighting, etc.

4 • Batch production – where a group of similar products are made at the same time. No group goes on to the next stage until all are ready
      3

• Flow production – where goods are made continually on a production line, with each stage adding to the product

• Job production – where a one-off product is made to a customer's own specification

      (25)

Case study 11 Clean4me

1 (a) • Less stress for partners
      1

• Bring specialist administration skills

• Help eliminate problems booking/scheduling

(b) Advantages

• Reach more customers
      2

• Cheaper form of advertising

• Online booking

Disadvantages

• Cost of setting up website

• Cost of maintaining/updating

• Training may be required

(c) • Have to share the profits
      2

• Greater chance of disagreements

• Didn't feel they needed more capital

• Decision making would take longer

Marks

2 • Private Limited Company 1
 • Public Limited Company

3 *(a)* Outsourcing – an arrangement where one company provides services, e.g. cleaning, for 1
 another company

 (b) • Will be cost-effective 2
 • Company will provide specialist equipment, employees
 • Can concentrate on core activities

4 *(a)* • Secondary sector – any business involved in the manufacture or production of goods 4
 • Primary sector – any business involved in the extraction of raw materials

 (b) • Secondary sector: e.g. car manufacturing 2
 • Primary sector: e.g. fishing

5 • Spreadsheet – prepare annual accounts, calculate wages, produce invoices, prepare cash 6
 flow statements
 • Database – set up customer database, staff database, mail merge
 • Word processing – standard letters, memos, reports, publicity materials

6 • Bank loan – interest is added 4
 • Bring in another partner – profits will be shared
 • Government grant – difficult to obtain
 • Hire purchase – asset does not belong to you until the last payment
 • Mortgage – property is secured against loan
 • Venture capitalist – they would want a share of the company profits

(25)

Case study 12 SuperJam

1 • Entrepreneur: the person who comes up with the business idea and takes the risk of 2
 starting the business
 • The role of an entrepreneur is to bring together the factors of production (land, labour,
 capital and enterprise). This person organises the finance for the business

2 Option 1
 • To gain more theoretical experience of running a business and managing the accounts 3

 Option 2
 • To reach a wider market
 • To gain more profits
 • To reduce the risk of failure

 Option 3
 • To become more well-known
 • To increase profits
 • To increase sales
 • To reach a new market

3 *(a)* • To highlight when a negative balance may occur 3
 • To give a business time to arrange alternative finance in advance

- To forecast periods of surplus cash
- To allow a business to make decisions – e.g. stop spending or invest in machinery
- To avoid liquidity problems
- To use to a secure bank loan
- To make comparisons between actual and projected figures

(b)
- Too much money tied up in stock   **2**
- Giving customers too long to pay
- Giving customers too much credit
- Borrowing too much money with high interest rates
- Owner taking out too many drawings
- Too much investment in capital items
- Poor sales

4 *(a)* Secondary sector – the sector where businesses manufacture products   **1**

    (b)
- Primary sector – businesses in this sector grow products or extract them from the ground, e.g. farming, mining   **4**
- Tertiary sector – businesses in this sector provide a service, e.g. hairdressers, banks

5
- Primary information – information that has been researched by the business for a specific purpose   **2**
- Secondary information – information that has been gathered from a previously published source

6
- Introduction – product is introduced into the market, sales are low and little or no profit is being made. No competition for this product   **3**
- Growth – sales and profits grow rapidly. Consumers become aware of the product
- Maturity – sales and profits reach their peak. Competition starts to emerge

7
- Retail outlets already have lots of customers   **1**
- Retail outlets are situated close to customers
- Retail outlets hold the stock so incur the storage costs
- Retail outlets have to employ staff to sell the product and pay for premises to sell it from

8
- Political factors – laws and decisions made by the Government, e.g. setting taxation rates   **4**
- Economic factors – inflation rate, exchange rates and interest rate changes
- Technological factors – advances in technology
- Environmental factors – changes in the environment, e.g. global warming
- Competitive factors – competitors decisions influence how organisations operate

Case study 13 Fifi and Ally

1
- Partnership   **2**
- A partnership is a business owned by 2–20 people, who share the workload, financing of the business and the profits

2 *(a)*
- Financial advice – e.g. drawing up Final Accounts   **2**
- Financial support – e.g. giving the business a loan/overdraft

Marks

- Business advice – e.g. drawing up a business plan, sourcing other people who could help the business (i.e. local suppliers, possible competitors, possible customers)

(b) • Other local businesses – suppliers to use, information on the local market   3
- Prince's Trust – may supply a grant, general business advice, writing business plan, legal advice
- Accountant – cash flow advice, Final Accounts advice, legal advice regarding the businesses accounts

3 (a) • Communication may become slow   1
- Decision making may be slowed down
- Could be expensive to pay lots of managers

(b) • Fiona and Alison cannot run the business effectively in a number of different locations   1
- It would help ease the worry of each store for Fiona and Alison

(c) • The business is expanding and needs more staff for the other stores   1
- It would ensure customers get a good service in each store

4 (a) • Induction training – training that is given to new employees to make them familiar with the business and their job   6
- On-the-job training – training that is given to employees while they are doing their job (e.g. sitting next to Nellie)
- Off-the-job training – training that is given to employees away from their normal job or away from their normal workplace

(b) • Lack of work completed while employees are being trained   2
- After being trained, employees may leave for another job
- After being trained, employees may demand higher wages

5 • Quality Control – a select number of products are checked at the end of production   3
- Quality Assurance – products are checked at certain points in the production process
- Quality Management – products are checked throughout the production process and no errors are tolerated. All staff are committed to ensuring quality. Customers are asked for a statement and all staff work towards achieving this
- Quality Circles – employees and managers sit and discuss where improvements can be made in the production process, which will improve the quality of the product
- Benchmarking – an organisation can look to the best producer in the industry and they will then try to copy their techniques to improve quality

6 • Email – communication can take place instantly from one computer to another. Information can reach people across the world very quickly, regardless of time differences   4
- Video-conferencing – allows people to see one another despite being in different locations around the world. Allows people to see each other's reactions, but does not involve the cost of flights or accommodation to facilitate this
- Mobile telephone – people can be contacted almost anywhere to discuss issues
- Networks – people can share information on a local area network (LAN) or wide area network (WAN)

(25)

Case study 14 Party Products

1 • Partnership – business owned by 2–20 people   2
- Private Limited Company – business owned by friends and family, shares sold privately

- Public Limited Company – business owned by shareholders who buy shares on the stock market

2 *(a)*
- Attract more customers
- Spreads the risk
- Become more competitive

1

(b)
- May not have skills to set up website
- Cost involved in setting up website
- Customer awareness may be low

1

(c)
- Would cost a lot of money
- Customers would need to be informed of move

1

3
- Political factors – Government may change legislation that may cause Clare to have to change the way she operates
- Economic factors – change in interest rates may increase the cost of any loans. Recession may mean a smaller demand for Clare's services
- Social factors – changes in society may affect the demand for the product, e.g. more ready meals/24-hour opening
- Technological factors – introduction of e-commerce will increase potential market but will mean companies will incur additional costs
- Environmental factors – global warming will affect weather conditions, e.g. more flooding. Companies may need to become more environmentally friendly to help reduce carbon emissions; this may cost additional money

3

4 Product
- Clare could change the name of her business
- Clare could update her premises
- Clare could offer additional services

6

Price
- Clare could use destroyer pricing to beat competitors
- Clare could use promotional pricing to attract additional customers
- Clare could increase prices to attract a different market segment

Promotion
- Clare could begin an advertising campaign on TV/newspapers
- Clare could begin special offers like buy one get one free
- Clare could offer a loyalty card/free gifts

5 *(a)*
- To survive financially
- To make a profit
- To increase sales
- To stay ahead of competitors

2

(b)
- Train staff to provide good-quality service
- Sell only good-quality products
- Do market research to find out customer wants

3

6 *(a)*
- Spreadsheet – a business might use this to complete its annual accounts on, using formulas to eliminate errors

2

- Database – a business might use this to store customer details on a database or to control their stock levels
- Email – a business might use this to contact suppliers or to send direct mailing to customers
- Presentation software – a business might use this as a marketing tool to show potential customers what the company offers; it might also use it for staff training purposes

(b) Costs

- The price of buying the hardware and the software   **4**
- The cost associated with installation and maintenance of the ICT
- Staff training
- Inefficiencies while staff are learning new system

Benefits

- Fewer errors/accidents
- Speed of information processing is increased
- Greater production
- Gives a competitive edge

(25)

Case study 15 The Farmhouse Restaurant

1
- Ask a partner to join the business   **2**
- Ask people to buy shares in the business
- Apply for a grant from the Government

2
- Prepare job analysis   **4**
- Prepare job description
- Prepare person specification
- Advertise job
- Send out application forms

3
- Advertise in newspapers, magazines, internet   **2**
- Send out vouchers
- Promotional prices

4
- Quality goods/service   **5**
- Good prices
- Delivering on time
- Give discounts
- Able to supply quantity required
- Dependable

5
- Satisfied customers   **4**
- Customers will return and tell others about the restaurant
- Increased profits owing to increase in custom
- Good reputation will result in high staff morale

6
- Balance Sheet: used to show the value of a business at a particular date   **4**
- Cash flow statement: used to show the movement of cash in and out of the business

- Cash budget: used to highlight periods when a negative cash/bank balance is expected, so that corrective action can be taken

7 • Primary sector: business involved in the extraction of raw materials, e.g. mining, farming, forestry   **4**

- Secondary sector: business involved in the manufacture of products, e.g. shipbuilding, construction, manufacturing

Solutions – Exam Style Questions

Marks

1 *(a)* (i) • Enable Apple's sales to increase   **3**
- Prevent the product going into decline
- Bring fresh interest into the product
- Stay ahead of competitors

(ii) • Change the name – e.g. Opal fruits → Starburst, Jif → Cif
- Promotions – buy one, get one free, 25% extra free
- Free gifts – e.g. Bluetooth headset, iTunes voucher
- Change the packaging – e.g. different-coloured iPods
- Change the price – lower the price

(b) • Share issue – sell shares on the stock exchange   **3**
- Bank loan – money lent from the bank that is repaid with interest
- Sale of assets – sell off any unused fixed assets
- Debenture issue – loans that are repaid on a specific date, interest is paid annually at a fixed rate
- Retained profits – reinvest existing profits

(c) (i) • Shareholders – profitability to see return on investment (dividends)   **6**
- Employees – profitability to ensure that they have job security
- The Government – to ensure that company is following regulations and paying the correct taxes

(ii) • Shareholders – they can vote at the AGM   **3**
- Employees – the standard of their work, industrial action
- The Government – can close company down or fine them

(d) • Zero defects   **4**
- Next person to work on product is seen as customer
- Total commitment from all employees and management
- Reduced wastage
- Perfect product

(e) • Number of employees   **3**
- Technology used
- The type of product
- The size of the market

(25)

2 *(a)* (i) • Horizontal integration – where firms producing the same products/services combine together   **6**

- Forward vertical integration – where a firm takes over a customer, e.g. a farmer takes over a butcher shop
- Backward vertical integration – where a firm takes over a supplier, e.g. a petrol station taking over an oil refinery
- Conglomerate integration (diversification) – where a firm takes over a business that operates in a completely different market

(ii) • To gain more profits   **2**
- To gain a bigger market share
- To become more well-known
- To avoid becoming the target for a takeover
- To reduce the risk of the business failing
- To reduce or eliminate competitors
- To take advantages of economies of scale

(b) Recruitment
- Carry out a job analysis   **6**
- Prepare a job description
- Prepare a person specification
- Advertise the job
- Post out application forms

Selection
- Analyse application forms/CVs
- Invite suitable candidates for tests
- Invite suitable candidates for interviews/carry out interviews
- Offer the most suitable candidate the job
- Inform unsuccessful candidates

(c) (i) Induction training   **1**

(ii) Costs
- Training is costly to provide   **6**
- While being trained, staff are less productive
- When trained, staff may ask for a pay rise
- When trained, staff may choose to leave and work elsewhere

Benefits
- Staff will become more skilled/competent at their job
- Allows the organisation to be more flexible
- Staff will be better motivated
- The organisation will be seen to be caring about employees – good reputation for firm
- Accidents in the workplace should decrease
- Quality of output should increase once fully trained
- Quantity of output should increase once fully trained

(d) • Advertise the new store in her current store   **4**
- Advertise on TV, radio, local newspaper
- Put fliers through doors
- Offer promotions to customers who visit the new branch – e.g. buy two items, get the third free

Marks

- Hold a fashion show, displaying supplies from the new branch
- Run a competition with entries from the new branch
- Give customers a voucher/discount coupon to visit the new branch

(25)

3 *(a)* • Development   **6**
    - Introduction
    - Growth
    - Maturity
    - Saturation
    - Decline

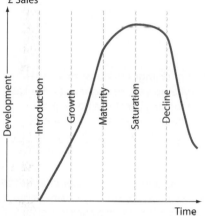

(b) • Improve the product   **3**
    - Change the packaging
    - Change name of product
    - Change price of product
    - Change advertising techniques

(c) (i) Strategic   **6**
    - Long-term decisions made by senior management concerning the aims and objectives of organisation

    Tactical
    - Medium-term decisions made by middle management about how to achieve the strategic decisions

    Operational
    - Decisions made by junior management concerning the day-to-day running of the organisation

(iii) Examples

    - Strategic: to sell more shares to public; to extend premises   **3**
    - Tactical: to buy more players from abroad
    - Operational: to change team members during football game

Marks

(d) • It could cause unrest in the workplace if workers are discriminated against because of their sex or race

  • Employers must abide by the various laws that have been passed protecting employees. If they do not do so they can face prosecution

2

(e) (i) • Stock control is important because if there is insufficient stock the business may be unable to satisfy customer demand. This will result in customers going elsewhere. Too much stock means money being tied up in stock. If stock is not used up it may deteriorate and as a result the business will lose money

2

(ii) • Maximum stock level – level of stock which business should hold in order to operate properly; level which stock should not rise above

  • Minimum stock level – level of stock that business should keep; stock should never fall below this level

  • Re-order stock level – level at which new stock should be ordered; it is calculated on the basis how much is used each day, the minimum stock held and the delivery time

3

(25)

4 (a) • Social influences: organisations must take account of changes in consumer tastes. Fashion changes from season to season and from year to year so organisations must make sure that their products suit the tastes of customers. Lifestyles have also changed. More women now work and this means they have less time to spend on preparing and cooking food. This has led to a variety of convenience foods and fast food outlets and organisations in this field must ensure they are meeting customer needs or they may lose custom to competitors

  • Political influences: the Government may decide to introduce new laws or change tax rates. Businesses must abide by any new laws or face prosecution, e.g. business must abide by the introduction of the minimum wage legislation. An increase in petrol tax may mean a threat to car sales

  • Economic influences: an increase in interest rates affects the amount of customer spending. When interest rates are low, customers are more likely to borrow and spend money; when interest rates are high, the opposite is the case

6

(b) • Time rate: employees are paid for the number of hours worked

  • Piece rate: employees are paid for the number of items they produce

  • Flat rate: employees are paid a set yearly salary which is divided into 12 equal monthly payments

  • Overtime: payment made when extra hours are worked. This is usually more than their normal hourly rate, e.g. time and a half

  • Bonus: an additional payment for increased productivity or if the organisation has had a successful year

  • Commission: used as an incentive payment to encourage employees to sell more. Usually calculated as a percentage of the product's sales value

6

(c) • If one product fails they have others to fall back on

  • Meets the needs of different customers

  • Allows entry into other markets

2

(d) • Sex Discrimination Act 1975: Men and women must be treated equally and fairly in the work place

  • Race Relations Act 1976: No discrimination should be made because of an employee's race, colour, nationality or ethnic origin

  • Health & Safety at Work Act 1974: Employers must provided a safe place of work for employees. Employees also have a duty to take care of their own health and safety and also that of other employees

6

Marks

- Disability Discrimination Act 1995: It is unlawful to discriminate against disabled employees. Organisations must make adjustments in the workplace to accommodate disabled employees
- National Minimum Wage Act 1999: This sets out the minimum wage that can be paid to employees

(e) (i)
- A brand is a tradename/design by which a product or group of products is identified, e.g. Cadbury, Kellogs, Heinz. Branding enables popular products to become well known   **1**

(ii) Advantages   **4**
- Easily recognised
- Usually good quality
- Customers are loyal to other goods in the brand
- High prices can be charged

Disadvantages
- It takes a long time to establish a brand
- If one good under the brand name suffers bad publicity, this can affect the whole range

(25)

5 *(a)* (i)   **6**

	Public Limited Company	**Sole trader**
Ownership	Owned by shareholders. Floated on the stock exchange	Owned by one person
Control	Controlled by the Board of Directors. Shareholders can vote on items at the Annual General Meeting	Controlled by the person who owns the business
Finance	Finance comes from shareholders, retained profits, bank loans/overdrafts, debentures, grants, trade credit	Owner's personal savings, retained profits, bank loans/overdrafts, grants, trade credit

(ii)
- To obtain more donations to serve their cause   **2**
- To make money to serve their cause
- To relieve poverty
- To provide a service

(b)
- Strategic – decisions taken by senior managers. These decisions affect businesses in the long term   **6**
- Tactical – decisions taken by senior/middle managers. These decisions are taken to achieve the strategic objectives of a business. These decisions affect businesses in the medium–long term
- Operational – decisions taken on a day-to-day basis. These decisions affect businesses in the short-term and are taken by lower level manager

(c)
- Quality Control – a select number of products are checked at the end of production   **8**
- Quality Assurance – products are checked at certain points in the production process
- Quality Management – products are checked throughout the production process and no errors are tolerated. All staff are committed to ensuring quality. Customers are asked for a statement and all staff work towards achieving this

- Quality Circles – employees and managers sit and discuss where improvements can be made in the production process, which will improve the quality of the product
- Benchmarking – an organisation can look to the best producer in the industry and they will then try to copy their techniques to improve quality

(d)
- Current assets – items the business owns that they are likely to keep for less than one year. The valuation of these items regularly changes   **3**
- Current liabilities – items the business owes in the short-term
- Fixed assets – items the business owns that they are likely to keep for more than one year. These items do not regularly change in value

(25)

6 *(a)*
- Private Limited Company – a company whose shares are owned privately and are not available for purchase on the Stock Market. It has a minimum of one shareholder. It is owned by the shareholder(s) and is run by a director or board of directors. Private Limited Companies must produce a Memorandum of Association and Articles of Association that state the company's details and who is responsible for it   **4**
- A Public Limited Company is a company whose shares are available for purchase on the Stock Market. There must be a minimum of two shareholders and a minimum of £50,000 share capital. A Memorandum of Association and Articles of Association must be produced outlining the details of the company, the responsibilities of the directors and the rights of shareholders

(b)
- Bank loan   **3**
- Sale of assets
- Retained profits
- Grant
- Personal savings

(c) (i)
- Primary sector: grow products or extract resources from the ground   **3**
- Secondary sector: manufactures products
- Tertiary sector: provide services

(ii)
- Primary: mining, farming   **3**
- Secondary: factories, construction, house building
- Tertiary: shops, hotels, hairdressing

(d) (i) Hierarchical   **4**
- Tall with many levels of management
- Long chain of command
- Decisions and instructions passed down from senior management
- Communication tends to be slow due to passing through so many levels

Flat
- Few layers of management
- Short chain of demand
- Quick decision making

(ii)
- Examples of hierarchical organisations: hospitals, banks, police force
- Examples of flat organisations: medical practice, accountants

(e)
- Benchmarking – comparing products produced against a more efficient producer. A business tries to understand its competitors' methods and to copy them   **6**
- Total Quality Management – quality is everybody's business. All staff are involved in ensuring that their individual work is of the highest quality. It is a system of doing things right first time. No errors are tolerated

Marks

- Quality Assurance – at various stages during the production process, products are checked to ensure they meet agreed quality standards. Any unsuitable products are discarded

(25)

7 *(a)* (i)
- Political   **5**
- Social
- Economic
- Competitive
- Technological

     (ii)
- Political – changes in law/taxation   **5**
- Social – changes in people's tastes and views
- Economic – recession/boom in economy
- Competitive – increasing amounts of competition
- Technological – advances in technology

(b) (i)
- Motivate staff   **4**
- Avoid industrial action
- Attract new employees to the organisation
- Employees remain loyal to the organisation

     (ii) Job description   **6**
- A document stating what is involved in the job, e.g. hours, duties
- Used to help write the person specification for the job

Reference
- A report written about a candidate for a job by their past employer
- Used by prospective new employer to show if the employee was a good worker etc.

Application form
- A form in which applicants give details to an employer of their personal details, qualifications and past work history
- Used to shortlist candidate for interviews

(c) (i) A legal document stating the terms and conditions of employment   **1**

     (ii)
- Job title   **4**
- Holiday entitlement
- Hours of work
- Notice required
- Salary

(25)

8 *(a)* The marketing mix is made up of the 4Ps: **4**
- Product – the good/service the organisation is selling
- Price – the amount of money that will be charged for the product/service
- Place – where the product/service will be made available to consumers
- Promotion – how the consumer will be made aware of the product/service

(b) • Introduction – product is introduced into the market, sales are low and little or no profit is being made. No competition for this product.

7

• Growth – sales and profits grow rapidly. Consumers become aware of the product.

• Maturity – sales and profits reach their peak. Competition starts to emerge.

• Decline – sales and profits are reduced. Product/service may be removed from the market. Market is saturated with competitors.

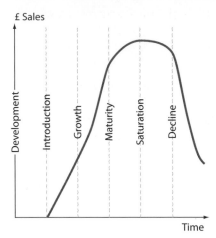

Diagram – 3 marks available: 1 mark for appropriate labelling of axis, 1 mark for appropriate curve, 1 mark for appropriate labelling of stages.

(c) JIT – this is a system that originated in Japan, which involves keeping stock levels to a minimum. Stock arrives just in time to be used in the production process. Little or no stock is stored

5

Costs

• If supplier is unreliable, the business may be left without stock

• Customers may be lost if the business is unable to supply goods

• Little time for quality control of raw materials

• Increased transport costs for smaller orders

• Bulk buying discounts may be lost

Benefits

• Storage costs are reduced

• Money is not tied up in stock

• Deterioration of stock is reduced

• Less vulnerable to changes in fashion/tastes

(d) (i) • Managers – interested to assess the performance of the business in comparison to previous years and/or competitors. Interested in reducing expenses and increasing profits with a view to increasing their salary/bonus

6

• Owners – interested to assess the performance of the business in comparison to previous years and/or competitors. Interested in ensuring their investment is still giving them a favourable return

• Employees – interested to ensure they are getting a fair pay deal from the organisation and to ensure job security

• Creditors – interested in the liquidity of an organisation to ensure the organisation will be able to pay its debt and will continue to give the creditor custom

• Community – interested in the business being successful to ensure jobs are available within the community

Marks

(ii) • Information is historical   **3**
- Ratios must be compared with something in order to be valuable
- Comparisons can only be made with ratios from firms of a similar size and nature
- Ratios do not take into account staff morale
- Ratios do not take into account external factors – e.g. recession
- Ratios do not take into account new product developments/declining products

(25)

9 *(a)* (i) • Benefits to employee: employee will know exactly his/her conditions of employment   **2**
- Benefits to employer: employer will be obliged to honour the contract of employment and will be protected with regard to dismissal procedures if employee is not suitable during period of trial

(ii) • Conditions of employment   **3**
- Hours of work
- Holiday entitlement
- Rate of pay and pay scale
- Notice required by both employee and employer
- Disciplinary procedures
- Grievance procedures

(b) (i) • Internal recruitment is when staff for a new post are recruited from within the organisation   **2**
- External recruitment is when staff for a new post are recruited from outwith the organisation

(ii) Advantages of internal recruitment   **4**
- Saves money on advertising position
- Boosts morale of staff
- Staff are already familiar with organisation
- Gives employees opportunity to develop their career

Advantages of external recruitment
- New ideas are brought into organisation
- Saves organisation from having to choose from a number of internal candidates
- Gives organisation the opportunity to attract a wide range of candidates with the right qualifications for the position

(c) (i) • Product   **4**
- Price
- Place
- Promotion

(ii) • Product – must meet needs of customer, otherwise sales will decrease   **4**
- Price – must be at right level: if higher than competitors, it will not sell; if too low, customers may feel that the product is cheap and inferior and not buy it
- Place – the product must be sold in the right place
- Promotion – customers must be aware of product and be persuaded to buy it through advertising and sales promotions

Marks

(d) • Written: appropriate to use for writing letters, sending emails, memos   **6**

 • Oral: appropriate to use when holding meetings, conversations and discussions

 • Pictorial: appropriate to use when passing on information that can be easily remembered, making documents more attractive and to emphasise certain points

 • Numerical: appropriate to use when making financial predictions and performing calculations

 • Graphical: appropriate to use when emphasising certain points or making comparisons

           (25)

10 (a) • Memorandum of Association   **4**

 • Articles of Association

(b) (i) • Sole trader – business owned by one person   **2**

 • Partnership – business owned by 2–20 people

(ii) Sole trader – advantages   **2**

 • Get to be your own boss

 • Get to keep the profits

 Sole trader – disadvantages

 • No-one to share the workload with

 • Unlimited liability

 Partnership – advantages

 • Increased specialisation

 • More capital

 Partnership – disadvantages

 • Decision making harder

 • Profits must be shared

(c) (i) • A diagram that shows the formal structure of an organisation.   **2**

 • It will show all the roles and responsibilities

(ii) • Functional grouping – when the business is arranged into specialist departments according to the particular function that they carry out   **2**

 • Examples: Finance, HR, Sales and Marketing, etc.

(iii) Advantages   **4**

 • Clear structure

 • Increase specialisation – staff become experts

 • Teamwork improves

 Disadvantages

 • Rivalry between departments

 • Communication barriers between departments

 • Introducing change may be more difficult

(d) (i) • Net profit percentage   **4**

$$\frac{\text{Net profit}}{\text{Sales}} \times 100$$

 • Gross profit percentage

$$\frac{\text{Gross profit}}{\text{Sales}} \times 100$$

Marks

- Return on capital employed

  $\dfrac{\text{Net profit}}{\text{Capital at start}} \times 100$

(ii)
- Information is historic **3**
- Like must be compared with like
- Do not account for external changes, e.g. recession/boom
- Do not take into account positive internal factors, e.g. highly trained and motivated staff

(e)
- Formal structure – an organisation with a formal structure has clear lines of responsibility **2**
  and authority. There are formal relationships between staff
- Informal structure – an organisation with an informal structure does not follow a
  strict hierarchy, with e.g. higher-level staff going out to play golf together. There are
  no formal relationships and informal communication takes place (grapevine)

(25)

11 (a) (i)
- Government – interested to make sure the school is spending their funding **8**
  appropriately and is providing a good education service
- Senior Management Team – interested in the school achieving good results,
  being placed highly in league tables, having a good reputation
- Teachers/employees – interested in job security and good conditions
- Pupils/parents – interested in receiving a good education and being in a safe
  environment
- Local community – interested in the school adding to the community – e.g. no
  litter, well trained pupils who could be employed/employ people in the
  community

(ii)
- Government – HMIe inspections, reduced funding **4**
- Senior Management Team – make decisions about the school's policy and
  practice
- Teachers/employees – leave to go to another post, absences from work, put on
  trips/extra curricular activities
- Pupils/parents – attend school, enrol children in the school, enrol children in
  another school
- Local community – complain to the council/school, make donations to the school

(b)
- Email – communication can take place instantly from one computer to another. **3**
  Information can reach people across the world very quickly, regardless of time
  differences
- Video-conferencing – allows people to see one another despite being in different
  locations around the world. Allows people to see each others reactions, but does not
  involve the cost of flights, accommodation to facilitate this
- Mobile telephone – people can be contacted almost anywhere to discuss issues
- Networks – people can share information on a local area network (LAN) or wide area
  network (WAN)

(c) Benefits **6**
- Increased productivity
- Less error/wastage
- More consistent quality
- Cheaper than employing more staff
- Can operate 24 hours, seven days per week – without breaks

Costs
- Costly to buy equipment, install and maintain
- Costly to train staff
- If machinery breaks down, production can stop
- Staff can feel de-motivated
- Viruses can corrupt data

(d)
- Race Relations Act – cannot discriminate against someone based on their race   **3**
- National Minimum Wage Act – employees must not be paid below a certain level (age dependent)
- Health and Safety at Work Act – employers must ensure the organisation is safe for employees. Employers have a duty of care for employees health and safety while in the workplace

(25)

12 (a)
- Current assets: items that a business owns and will keep for less than a year   **3**
- Long-term liabilities: debts that are not due to be paid for more than 12 months
- Gross profit: profit made by a business before expenses have been deducted

(b) (i)
- Negative cash flow: the business is experiencing difficulties paying its day-to-day expenses   **1**

(ii)
- Sell any unnecessary fixed assets   **3**
- Encourage customers to pay their bills on time
- Offer discounts to encourage cash sales and reduce stock levels
- Arrange credit terms with suppliers
- Look for cheaper suppliers

(c)
- Bank manager: financial advice, loan   **4**
- Lawyer: legal advice on setting up business
- Prince's Trust: general advice on grants and training available
- Local businesses: information about the area where business is expected to be set up and information on trade in that area

(d)
- Customers: they are interested in the service that the bank offers. Interest rates and bank charges are important to them and they will want the best possible rates or they may take their custom elsewhere   **6**
- Employees: they are interested in their conditions of service. They are interested in their career prospects and job security
- Suppliers: they are interested in the success of the bank as they wish to receive payment for the goods they supply as quickly as possible

(e)
- Setting a low price to attract customers to the product. As the product becomes established the price is then increased   **3**
- Setting a high price initially – usually for a new product. As competitors enter the market the price is lowered
- Used to increase sales in the short term by lowering the price and attracting customers. Supermarkets do this all the time. They lower the price of some products in the hope that customers will also buy other items not on promotion

(f)
- Good-quality goods   **5**
- Reliability
- Delivering on time
- Competitive prices

Marks

- Discounts for prompt payment/buying in bulk
- Credit facilities

(25)

13 *(a)*
- Provide training **3**
- Provide safety clothing, e.g. hard hat
- Keep an accident book
- Provide first aid supplies

(b) Costs **6**
- Cost of course
- Subsistence expenses
- Cost of staff cover
- Inefficiencies while training occurs
- Loss of production

Benefits
- Increased production levels
- Staff improve their skills
- Increased employee motivation
- Improved quality
- Less accidents occur in the workplace

(c)
- Labour intensive production – when organisations use a workforce rather than machinery to carry out production **4**

Labour intensive production provides:
- a unique product
- a high-quality product
- a product for which premium price can be charged
- a product that fits customer specifications

However, capital intensive production may be more efficient as machinery can operate 24 hours a day.

(d) (i)
- Internal growth – increasing sales, hiring additional employees **8**
- Horizontal growth – two firms that produce the same service merging together
- Vertical growth – two firms at different stages of production joining together (forwards or vertical)
- Diversification – a company taking over a completely different business to their original one

(ii)
- Email – enables mail to be sent from one electronic mailbox to another in seconds **4**
- Video-conferencing – this enables people in one location to talk face-to-face with people in another location without the need to travel
- Fax – allows an exact copy of a document to be transmitted through the telephone lines in seconds
- Mobile phone/WAP – allows people to be contacted very easily wherever they are

(25)

Marks

14 *(a)* (i) • Political – laws and decisions made by the Government, e.g. setting taxation rates   **8**
- Economic – inflation rate, exchange rates and interest rate changes
- Social – changes in the population, e.g. an ageing population in the UK and changes in attitudes/lifestyles, e.g. people have more leisure time
- Technological – advances in technology
- Environmental – changes in the environment, e.g. global warming
- Competitive – competitors' decisions influence how organisations operate

(ii) • Political – organisations will need to abide by these laws and decisions   **4**
- Economic – may result in more sales and profits if the economy is experiencing a boom or lower sales and profits if the economy is experiencing a recession
- Social – organisations will need to cater for these changes, e.g. produce products for an ageing population
- Technological – organisations need to keep up with advances in technology
- Environmental – organisations may be put under pressure to become more environmentally friendly
- Competitive – organisations must stay ahead of competitors or react to counter decisions competitors make

(b) • Reliability – can you depend on the supplier to deliver on time and to deliver the goods the organisation requires?   **5**
- Price – is the price appropriate for the quality?
- Quality – is the quality of the goods acceptable for the organisation?
- Quantity – is the supplier able to supply the amount of goods the organisation requires?
- Location – is the supplier located close to the organisation to reduce deliver costs?
- Credit terms – does the supplier offer any discounts for buying in bulk or being a regular customer?

(c) • Quality Circles – employees and managers sit and discuss where improvements can be made in the production process, which will improve the quality of the product. This influences the quality as improvements are constantly being discussed and suggestions come from people on the shop-floor who know best how to improve the production process   **4**
- Benchmarking – an organisation can look to the best producer in the industry and then try to copy their techniques to improve quality. Setting a benchmark can be motivational for staff as they have a target to achieve and a clear standard to copy

(d) • Offer discounts and promotions to encourage more sales   **4**
- Reduce the amount of stock held as this ties up cash flow
- Sell fixed assets the business does not need
- Encourage debtors to pay
- Arrange credit facilities with suppliers
- Owners should take less drawings
- Organise additional finance, e.g. bank loan, take on a partner, float on stock exchange

(25)

15 *(a)* (i) • Decrease profitability   **3**
- Decrease market share
- Damage company image
- Loss of customers

(ii) • Increase profitability   **3**

Marks

- Relocate business
- Merge with another company

(b)
- Written – information in the form of text: can keep a copy to refer back to **10**
- Oral – verbal information: instant response
- Pictorial – information in the form of pictures: more attractive way to display documents
- Numerical – information in the form of numbers: businesses may be able to make forecasts of future financial positions
- Graphical – information in the form of graphs and charts: makes it easier to make comparisons

(c) Costs
- May be expensive to set up **5**
- Lose personal contact with customers

Benefits
- Can sell 24 hours a day
- Will be cheaper than having a shop, fittings, etc
- Reaches a world-wide market
- Can collect customer details to build a database for marketing purposes

(d) The Data Protection Act 1998

Points covered
- Information must be kept up to date **4**
- Information must not be held for longer than necessary
- Information must be processed lawfully
- Information must only be held for the purpose registered
- Information must not be passed on to third parties without consent

(25)

16 (a)
- Increase sales **3**
- Reduce expenses
- Find a cheaper supplier

(b)
- Trading Profit and Loss Account **2**
- Balance Sheet

(c) (i) Make it unlawful to discriminate against someone on the grounds of age. New national retirement age of 65 **1**

(ii)
- Health and Safety at Work Act **6**
- Equal Pay Act
- National Minimum Wage Act
- Sex Discrimination Act
- Race Relations Act
- Data Protection Act

(d)
- Works councils are made up of an equal number of representatives from employees and management. At meetings of the works council, people can discuss matters affecting the business, especially the impact they have on the workers **2**
- Trade unions are organisations set up to represent workers' interests in such matters as pay and working conditions

Marks

(e) • Full-time – working a full week, for example Monday to Friday, 9 am to 5 pm   **6**
   • Part-time – working fewer hours than those with full-time contracts, for example, 15 hours per week
   • Flexi-time – when employees can choose the start and end times for their working day but they must be at work during core times in the day

(f) (i) • Good pay   **3**
      • Bonuses
      • Training opportunities
      • Promotion opportunities
      • Team-building exercises

   (ii) • Reduces staff absenteeism/turnover   **2**
       • Easier to recruit new employees
       • Gives company a good image

(25)

17 (a) • Advertise on TV, radio, local newspaper   **3**
    • Put fliers through doors
    • Offer promotions to customers who visit the shop – e.g. buy two items, get the third free
    • Hold an art exhibition for local/famous artists
    • Run a competition with entries from shop
    • Give customers a voucher/discount coupon to visit the shop
    • Offer art lessons in the shop
    • Reduce prices

(b) • Desk research – where the researcher uses secondary information. This information was published for a different reason, but is still useful. Example: Government statistics, trade journals, Final Accounts   **6**
   • Field research – where the researcher goes out into the market and obtains information for a specific purpose. Example: questionnaires, interviews, consumer audits, hall test

(c) (i) • Oral – verbal information   **5**
      • Written – information in the form of text
      • Graphical – information in the form of charts and graphs
      • Quantitative – information that is expressed in figures
      • Qualitative – information that is an expression that involves judgements/opinions

   (ii) • Timely – available when you need it and up-to-date   **5**
       • Accurate – correct
       • Concise – to the point
       • Cost effective – the cost to gain this information should not outweigh its value to the firm
       • Appropriate – useful for the purpose
       • Available – easy for the organisation to obtain
       • Complete – nothing is missing

(d) (i) • Identify the problem   **4**
      • Identify the objectives
      • Gather information
      • Analyse information
      • Devise possible solutions

Marks

- Select the best solution
- Communicate the decision
- Implement the decision
- Evaluate the decision

(ii) • Can be time-consuming to go through all the stages   2
- Can stifle the decision-maker's creativity
- Can be difficult to come up with a range of solutions
- Can be difficult to choose from a range of solutions

(25)

18 *(a)* (i) • Conglomerate integration – businesses operating in different markets merge   1

(ii) • Horizontal integration – businesses producing the same type of product or offering the same service merge   4
- Vertical integration – businesses at different stages of production in the same industry merge

(b) • Induction training: given to new members of staff. It covers background information about the organisation, department procedures, tasks involved in the job, and health and safety issues   6
- On-the-job training: staff are trained at their place of work
- Off-the-job training: takes place outwith the workplace, at a college or training centre

(c) Important decisions are made on information gathered. If this is not accurate or up to date, wrong decisions could be made, which may result in the business losing money and customers   2

(d) (i) To show how much profit or loss a business has made over a period of time. It shows how much money has come into business and how much has been spent   2

(ii) • Gross profit percentage: used to measure the profit from buying and selling stock   6
- Net profit percentage: used to measure profit made after the business has paid all its expenses
- Return on capital employed: used to measure the return on the capital invested into the business by owner or shareholders

(e) • Database: allows hospital to store patient records; allows hospital to sort records, search for specific information and produce reports   4
- Spreadsheet: allows hospital to perform calculations, produce 'what if' scenarios and produce graphs and charts of its calculations
- PowerPoint: allows hospital to make presentations
- Word processing: allows hospital to create and edit text, e.g. letters, memos, etc. to send out to patients and medical centres

(25)

Marks

19 *(a)*

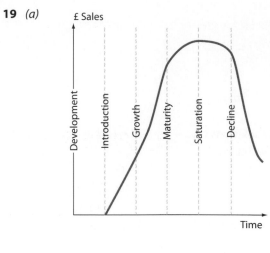

£ Sales

Development | Introduction | Growth | Maturity | Saturation | Decline

Time

4

(b) • Product – adapt packaging, new and improved versions
 • Place – sell in more places, e.g. on internet
 • Price – reduce price, promotional pricing
 • Promotion – begin a new advertising campaign

4

(c) • Customer loyalty
 • Can charge high prices
 • Easier to launch new products
 • Instanty recongnisable

4

(d) (i) • Batch production – where sets of similar goods are produced in batches. One batch is not started until the next is completed

2

 (ii) • Job production – creating a unique product to customer specifications, e.g. a wedding dress
 • Flow production – the continous production of identical products along a production line, where value is added at each stage, e.g. cars

4

(e) • Manufacturer → Consumer
 • Manufacturer → Wholesaler → Retailer → Consumer
 • Manufacturer → Retailer → Consumer

3

(f) Overstocking
 • Too much money tied up in stock
 • High storage costs
 • High chance of goods deteriorating

Understocking
 • Unable to meet customer demand
 • Loss of customer loyalty

4

(25)

20 *(a)* (i) • Attainment tests – give candidates the opportunity to demonstrate skills in a particular area
 • Aptitude tests – test candidates' natural ability
 • Intelligence tests (IQ) – measure candidates' mental ability
 • Medical tests – assess candidates physical ability to do the job
 • Psychometric tests – analyse candidates' personality and traits

6

(ii) Costs   **8**
- Training is costly to provide
- While being trained, staff are less productive
- When trained, staff may ask for a pay rise
- When trained, staff may choose to leave and work elsewhere

Benefits
- Staff will become more skilled/competent at their job
- Allows the organisation to be more flexible
- Staff will be more motivated
- The organisation will be seen to be caring about employees – good reputation for firm
- Accidents in the workplace should decrease
- Quality of output should increase once fully trained
- Quantity of output should increase once fully trained

(b)
- Debtors – people that owe Jason money   **3**
- Creditors – people that Jason owes money to
- Working capital – the difference between Jason's current assets and his current liabilities

(c) (i)
- De-layering – removing a level of management from the business to flatten the structure   **2**
- Downsizing – removing certain areas of the organisation's activities by closing factoring/merging parts together

(ii) De-layer   **6**
- To improve communication lines
- To allow decisions to be made faster
- To empower staff
- To cut management costs
- To make the business more flexible in terms of reacting to changes in the market

Downsize
- To cut costs
- To increase profit levels
- To empower staff
- To become more competitive in the market

    (25)

21 (a)
- Job application form: form filled in by people applying for a job. Applicants have to answer set questions contained in the application form   **6**
- Job description: description of the job, where it is located, tasks, duties and responsibilities involved; conditions of service; holiday entitlement and hours to be worked
- Person specification: description of the type of person that would be suitable including qualifications, experience and personal qualities required

(b)
- Free samples   **3**
- Credit facilities
- Buy one, get one free
- Vouchers/coupons
- Competitions
- Demonstrations in store

(c) (i) • To find out what customers think of its product   **2**
 • To find out how effective its advertising is
 • To provide information about the nature and size of its target market

    (ii) • Personal interview: involves face-to-face interview where questions are asked and responses noted   **4**
 • Telephone survey: involves a researcher telephoning people at home and asking questions
 • Postal survey: people are sent questionnaires through the post asking them to fill them in and return them

(d) • To advertise their goods   **3**
 • To sell their goods
 • To find out information

(e) • Finance department: payment of wages; preparation of financial statements; analysis of financial information   **4**
 • Human resources department: recruitment of staff; staff training; health and safety issues

(f) • Availability of land   **3**
 • Choice of labour
 • Capital available
 • Government restrictions

                                                                              (25)

22 *(a)* • Develops a business idea   **4**
 • Combines the factors of production
 • Takes financial risks
 • Responsible for decision making

   (b) (i) • Mortgage – a long-term loan for property   **4**
 • Grant – money given by an organisation that does not need to be repaid
 • Bank loan – money borrowed from the bank that can be repaid in regular fixed installments
 • Debenture – a long-term loan where debenture holders are creditors and not owners of a company

    (ii) • Mortgage – large amount raised / property secured against it
 • Grant – money does not have to be paid back / might not be a large enough sum; difficult to get
 • Bank loan – high interest rates / repaid in installments
 • Debenture – ownership is not diluted as the debenture holders are creditors to the firm / a fixed rate of interest must be paid each year

                                                                              8

   (c) (i) • Strike – employees do not attend work   **6**
 • Sit-in – a method of protesting where the employees sit in the workplace and refuse to move, hence disturbing operations
 • Work to rule – employees do no more than is required by their contract
 • Go slow – employees reduce their output
 • Boycott – employees refuse to take part in some aspect in the workplace

Marks

(ii) • Demotivates workers 3
- Damages reputation
- Loss of sales
- Loss of production

(25)

23 *(a)* (i) • Capital intensive production – production that relies heavily on machinery 2
- Labour intensive production – production that relies heavily on people rather than machinery

(ii) Advantages 6
- Product is made to a standard level at all times
- Machinery can work 24 hours, seven days, without needing breaks
- Machinery can produce high numbers in a short period of time
- Can be helpful when labour costs are high

Disadvantages
- Can be costly to install and maintain machinery
- If breakdowns occur, production may have to stop
- Individual, one-off jobs cannot be easily catered for
- Employees find it a boring job – less motivated

(b) • Quality Control – a select number of products are checked at the end of production 4
- Quality Assurance – products are checked at certain points in the production process
- Benchmarking – an organisation can look to the best producer in the industry and try to copy their techniques to improve quality
- Quality Circles – employees and managers sit and discuss where improvements can be made in the production process, which will improve the quality of the product

(c) Advantages 4
- Owner can keep all the profits
- Owner has full control of the business
- Easy to set up

Disadvantages
- Owner has unlimited liability
- Finance is difficult to obtain
- Owner has no-one to share decision making or problems with

(d) (i) • If they feel they are being treated unfairly at work 1
- If they are unhappy with their pay
- When employees and employers cannot agree

(ii) • Sit-in – employees stay in the workplace but do not do any work 8
- Overtime ban – employees refuse to work any extra hours
- Work to rule – employees only undertake duties stated in their contract of employment
- Go slow – employees work, but at a very slow rate
- Strike – employees refuse to enter the workplace

(25)

Marks

24 *(a)* • Land: the natural resources that businesses use   8
• Labour: the workers of the organisation
• Capital: the machinery, equipment, etc. that an organisation owns and controls and the money invested in the business by the owners
• Enterprise: the business ideas of the owner on how best to use all the factors of production

(b) (i) • Loan from bank   3
• Grant from Government
• Owner's savings
• Allowing people to buy shares in business

(ii) Loan from bank   6
• Advantage: fairly easy to obtain
• Disadvantage: interest is charged on the loan

Grant from Government
• Advantage: you do not normally have to pay this back
• Disadvantage: certain restrictions are often put on a grant, e.g. give jobs to unemployed

Owner's savings
• Advantage: readily available
• Disadvantage: no guarantee that he will get this back

Buying shares in business
• Advantage: large sums of money can be raised
• Disadvantage: shareholders will have a share in business. They will also expect a good return for their investment

(c) • Outsourcing: when work is sent out of the organisation to be carried out by an outside firm   3
• Span of control: the number of people a supervisor/manager has under his/her control
• De-layering: when certain layers of management are removed from organisation

(d) • Allows stock to be updated on a regular basis and amendments to be made easily and quickly   2
• Enables information to be searched and reports produced to assist decision making

(e) • Flexi-time: employees can start and finish work at different times as long as they complete a set number of hours every week   3
• Part-time: employees do not work for a full week, e.g. mornings, afternoons or a set number of days per week
• Temporary: employees do not have a permanent position and are only employed when required

(25)

25 *(a)* (i) • A structure with few levels of management   2
• Small organisations tend to have flat structures

(ii) • Faster communication   5
• Faster decision making
• Workers empowered
• Reduced expenses as fewer management salaries
• Information will not get lost/distorted
• Can respond to market changes more quickly

Marks

(b) (i) • Will provide positive publicity   **2**
       • Will attract customers

  (ii) • They are gauranteed a quality service   **1**
       • Can trust the independent views of Tommy

  (iii) • BS5750   **2**
       • Lion Mark
       • Kitemark
       • CE Mark

(c) (i) • To increase profits   **3**
       • To increase market share
       • To be socially responsible

  (ii) • Horizontal integration   **6**
       • Backwards vertical integration
       • Forward vertical integration
       • Organic growth
       • Conglomerate integration
       • Mergers
       • Takeovers
       • Horizontal integration – when a business joins with another business at the same stage of production/in the same market
       • Backwards vertical integration – when a business joins with a another business a stage behind in production
       • Forward vertical integration – when a business joins with another business a stage ahead in production
       • Organic growth – when a firm grows naturally through increasing in size, e.g. increasing sales
       • Conglomerate integration – when a company joins with another unrelated company; this is a type of diversification
       • Mergers – joining with another company
       • Takeovers – when one company purchases another

  (iii) • Email – enables mail to be sent from one electronic mailbox to another in seconds   **4**
       • Video-conferencing – this enables people in one location to talk face-to-face with people in another location without the need to travel
       • Fax – allows an exact copy of a document to be transmitted through the telephone lines in seconds
       • Internet – allows customers to be reached world-wide

                                                         (25)

26 *(a)* (i) Advantages   **4**
       • Security is improved as all the stock is in the one area and can be controlled by specialists
       • Specialist staff can be employed to maintain stocks – improved efficiency
       • Cheaper storage costs, than a number of smaller storage units

      Disadvantages
       • Stock is not close to hand for all departments/stores
       • Stock may be ordered that is not often required due to lack of knowledge of specific department needs

- If all stock is located in the one area and a fire/disaster happens, the entire firm's stock will be damaged

(ii) • Maximum stock level – the highest amount of stock an organisation should hold, based on storage space, usage and finance available **4**
- Minimum stock level – the level of that stock should not fall below in case of reduced output
- Re-order level – the point at which new stock should be ordered
- Re-order quantity – the amount of stock that should be re-ordered to take the level back to the maximum level

(iii) Overstocking **4**
- High storage costs
- High security costs
- Too much money tied up unnecessarily
- Risk that stock could become out of date/deteriorate before use

Understocking
- Business may run out of stock
- Business may have to stop production
- Customers may go elsewhere
- Business may get a poor reputation
- Business may be unable to deal with unexpected increases in demand

(b) • Gross profit percentage – to measure the profit made by buying and selling stock **3**
- Return on capital employed – to measure the return the investors gain on the money they put in
- Current ratio/working capital ratio – to show the business's ability to pay its short-term debts

(c) • The ability of employees to perform their role **2**
- The quality of the information available within the business
- The availability of up-to-date ICT
- The ability of the management team to make effective decisions

(d) • Political – organisations will need to abide by these laws and decisions **8**
- Economic – may result in more sales and profits if the economy is experiencing a boom or less sales and profits if the economy is experiencing a recession
- Social – organisations will need to cater for these changes – e.g. produce products for an ageing population
- Technological – organisations need to keep up with advances in technology
- Environmental – organisations may be put under pressure to become more environmentally friendly
- Competitive – organisations must stay ahead of competitors or react to counter decisions competitors make

(25)

27 (a) (i) • Make comparisons **3**
- Forecast information
- Identify differences
- Find solutions to aid improvements

Marks

 (ii) • Profitability – calculate how profitable a firm is   **6**
   • Liquidity – calculate the firm's ability to pay short-term debts
   • Efficiency – calculate how well a firm is using its resources

 (iii) • Do not account for external factors   **2**
   • Do not show staff motivation/turnover
   • Like must be compared with like

(b) (i) • Providing staff training   **5**
   • Bonuses
   • Fringe benefits
   • Team-building events
   • Praise
   • Access to promotions

 (ii) • Poor-quality work   **3**
   • Absenteeism
   • Loss of output
   • Not working well with other colleagues

(c) • Full-time – working from 9 to 5 for a full week (e.g. 35 hours)   **6**
  • Part-time – working fewer hours than full time (e.g. 20 hours)
  • Blue collar workers – also referred to as unskilled workers, carry out manual/repetitive tasks
  • White collar workers – also referred to as skilled workers or professionals
  • Senior managers – top-level managers who are responsible for making strategic decisions
  • Junior managers – are lower-level managers who are responsible for the operational decisions

                    (25)

28 *(a)* (i) • National Insurance   **2**
   • Income tax

 (ii) • Keeping financial records   **2**
   • Paying bills

 (iii) • Marketing – advertising, market research   **6**
   • Human Resources – training, recruitment, selection
   • Operations – maintaining quality, stock control, production of goods
   • Administration – keeping records, photocopying
   • Research and Development – looking for ways to produce new products or improve existing products

(b) • Develops the individual's skills   **4**
  • Increased job satisfaction
  • Increased motivation
  • Breaks down the barriers between departments
  • Everyone will have same level of responsibility

(c) (i) • Passwords   **3**
   • Anti-virus software
   • Firewalls
   • Different levels of access to computer systems

Marks

(ii) The Data Protection Act 1998   **1**

(iii) • Staff training   **3**
- Installation costs
- Job losses
- Decrease in staff motivation
- Data corruption

(d) • Lead time – time taken from ordering goods to receiving delivery   **4**
- Economies of scale – the benefits a business gains from being larger
- Inventory – a list of stock items
- Automation – when operations systems are controlled by a computer

(25)

29 (a) (i) • Desk research – where the researcher uses secondary information. This information was published for a different reason, but is still useful. Examples: Government statistics, trade journals, Final Accounts   **6**
- Field research – where the researcher goes out into the market and obtains information for a specific purpose. Examples: questionnaires, interviews, consumer audits, hall test

(ii) • Random sampling – people are chosen from pre-selected lists (e.g. electoral roll) and are called randomly. If the person is not available, the interviewer must keep trying to get them to gain their views   **4**
- Quota sampling – the interviewer is given a list of instructions as to what numbers and types of people they should interview – e.g. dependent on age, sex, social status
- Stratified sampling – a sample group is identified based on the make-up of the population as a whole – e.g. if 10% of the population is in socio-economic group AB, then the group sampled must be made up of 10% from the AB grouping

(b) • Price discrimination – pricing the product/service differently at different times of the year   **4**
- Penetration pricing – setting the initial prices low to penetrate the market, once the business has a customer base the price will rise again in line with competitors
- Destroyer pricing – prices are set artificially low to force competitors out of the market. Once competitors have been destroyed, the business raises its prices
- Promotional pricing – where the business reduces its prices for a short time
- Premium pricing – setting the price high to give the product/service an exclusive feel
- Loss leaders – setting the price of some items at an unprofitable level to encourage buyers to think all products/services will be low priced
- Competitive pricing – setting the price at the same level as competitors in the market

(c) • Equal Pay Act – all employees should receive the same pay for jobs of equal worth   **8**
- Sex Discrimination Act – organisations cannot discriminate on the grounds of sex
- Race Relations Act – organisations cannot discriminate on the grounds of race, colour or nationality
- Employment Equality Regulations – organisations cannot discriminate on the grounds of religion or age
- National Minimum Wage Act – organisations must pay employees a minimum rate (age dependent)

(d) • Trade unions – to represent employees views to management and negotiate on their behalf   **3**

Marks

- Industrial action – actions employees may take if they cannot reach agreement with management
- ACAS (Advisory, Conciliation and Arbitration Service) – a Government body that helps in disputes between employers and employees, where agreement could not be reached

(25)

30 *(a)*
- Random sampling: People are pre-selected from a list such as a telephone directory. The interviewer makes a number of calls on people chosen from the list until he/she is able to get their views
- Quota sampling: The researcher is told the number and type of people to interview. It is the researcher's job to find the people required

2

(b) Employees

4
- They will feel more confident in their job as they have been trained to do it
- This should also increase motivation and also production

Organisation
- A happy workforce should result because staff know what they are doing
- Well-trained staff give customers confidence
- Well-trained staff boost the reputation of an organisation

(c) (i) Advantages

4
- Someone to share workload with
- Able to take time off
- May be in better position to borrow money if needed
- Can take on more business due to extra help

Disadvantages
- No longer in sole charge of business
- Profits will be required to be shared
- Partnership Agreement must be drawn up
- Will not be able to make all decisions – must consult partner

(ii) Role of entrepreneur – to undertake a commercial venture often at personal financial risk

2

(d)
- Input – the raw materials, equipment and labour used to produce a product/service
- Process – actual making of the product or providing the service using the above
- Output – the final product/service

3

(e)
- Competitive pricing – charging the same price for products as similar organisations in the market
- Loss leaders – charging a low unprofitable price for a range of products to entice customers into your store hoping that once they are in the store they will buy other normally priced products
- Price discrimination – charging different prices for products according to the time of day. Supermarkets charge a much lower price in the evening for bread, cakes, etc. Holiday firms charge a different price for the same holiday according to the time of booking

3

(f) (i)
- Go on strike – refuse to work
- Work to rule – only undertake tasks contained in their job description
- Refuse to do any overtime – refuse to work extra hours
- Arrange a sit-in – remain at their place of work but refuse to do any work
- Go slow – produce work at a much slower rate than normal

4

Marks

(ii) • Corporate culture: the atmosphere and work ethics within an organisation   **3**

Evidence
- The behaviour of staff
- Attitude of staff to work
- Dress code of staff (may wear a certain uniform)

(25)

31 *(a)* Sole trader   **9**
- Owned by one person
- Unlimited Liability
- Can be difficult to raise finance
- Can keep all the profits

Partnership
- Owned by 2–20 people
- Unlimited liability
- Profits and losses are shared
- Will draw up a contract of employment

Public Limited Company
- Minimum start-up capital of £50,000 required
- Has limited liability
- Shares are sold on stock market
- Owners are called shareholders and they receive a dividend

(b) • Provide a service   **4**
- Relieve poverty
- Advance education
- Raise money for good cause
- Attract more volunteers

(c) (i) • Maintenance of records – a database could be constructed to store and sort information   **3**
- Marketing a new product – DTP could be used to produce flyers, Internet could be used to advertise worldwide, email could be used for direct marketing
- Provision of information – email could be used to send information, PowerPoint could be used to present information, DVPs could be used to display information

(ii) • Jobs may change   **3**
- Training may be required
- Some employees may lose their jobs
- Staff may become demotivated

(d) (i) • Increase advertising   **3**
- Try to keep expenses to minimum
- Keep good records
- Prepare a budget
- Find suitable sources of finance, e.g. overdraft
- Impose tight credit control

Marks

(ii) • Information is historic   **3**
  • Like has to be compared with like
  • Does not take into account external factors

(25)

32 *(a)* (i) • Job production – where a one-off product is made to a customer's own   **6**
specification
  • Batch production – where a group of similar products are made at the same time;
no group goes on to the next stage until all are ready
  • Flow production – where goods are made continually on a production line, with
each stage adding to the product

(ii) Job – advantages   **6**
  • Customers' specific requirements can be met
  • Highly motivational for staff to work on different jobs
  • High prices can be charged

Job – disadvantages
  • Expensive in terms of staff wages
  • A wide variety of tools/machinery is required
  • Lead times can be lengthy

Batch – advantages
  • Reduced need for highly skilled and trained staff
  • Machinery can be more standardised, which again reduces costs

Batch – disadvantages
  • If batches are small, costs will still be high
  • Staff may find it repetitive – less motivated
  • Machinery may lie idle between batches

Flow – advantages
  • Standard quality levels can be achieved more consistently
  • Machines can work 24 hours, seven days a week, without breaks
  • Production levels can be high
  • Labour costs are reduced

Flow – disadvantages
  • Staff find it repetitive and boring – less motivated
  • If machinery breaks down, production may stop completely
  • Installations and maintenance of machinery incurs high costs
  • Does not allow for individual customer requests to be met

(b) • Point of sale materials – free displays, posters   **4**
  • Dealer loaders – buy ten items, get two free
  • Sale or return – if the retailer does not sell the items, it can return them to the
manufacturer
  • Dealer competitions – retailer may be entered into a competition
  • Staff training – the manufacturer may pay for retail staff training
  • Credit facilities – retailers can take time to pay the manufacturer for the goods

(c) (i) Span of control – the number of subordinates that are working under any supervisor/   **1**
manager

(ii) Narrow span of control   **2**

- Managers supervise a smaller number of staff
- Manager is able to supervise staff more closely

Wide span of control

- Manager supervises a larger number of staff
- Manager must delegate many tasks so staff need to be capable of dealing with it
- Staff may be required to take on more responsibility and make decisions on their own
- Manager has less time to supervise employees' work closely

(d)
- Strategic – decisions taken by senior managers. These decisions affect businesses in the long term. Examples: to expand, to increase profit levels by 25%   **6**
- Tactical – decisions taken by senior/middle managers. These decisions are taken to achieve the strategic objectives of a business and affect businesses in the medium to long term. Examples: to arrange suitable premises for the expansion, to increase product range to encourage profit levels to rise
- Operational – decisions taken on a day-to-day basis. These decisions are taken by lower-level managers and affect businesses in the short term. Example: to cover for an absent member of staff

     (25)

33 (a)
- Patients: they can complain about the amount of time they have to wait for hospital appointments   **6**
- Government: they can restrict the amount of funding they give
- Employees: they can take industrial action if they are unhappy about conditions of service

(b)
- Labour intensive production: relies on the workforce rather than machinery to carry out tasks   **2**
- Capital intensive production: relies on machinery and automation to produce goods

(c) (i)
- Identify the problem   **5**
- Identify the objectives
- Identify any constraints
- Gather information required
- Analyse the information gathered
- Devise possible solutions
- Select the best solution
- Communicate the decision
- Implement the decision
- Evaluate decision made

(ii)
- Quality of information available   **4**
- Experience of decision maker
- The ability of the decision maker to take risks
- Personal interest of the decision maker
- The finance available to carry out decision

(d) (i) Trading Profit and Loss Account   **2**
- Sales
- Gross profit
- Net profit

Marks

    (ii) Balance Sheet   **2**

- Fixed assets
- Current assets
- Drawings

(e) (i)
- Tall organisation structure: an organisation that has many levels of management. Decisions and instructions are passed down by senior staff. There tend to be many departments in this type of structure with a manager in charge of each department   **2**
- Flat organisation structure: an organisation with few levels of management. There are fewer managers and each department tends to have more independence. This structure is suitable for small to medium-sized organisations

    (ii)
- Tall organisation: large banks, e.g. Royal Bank of Scotland   **2**
- Flat organisation: local health centre

(25)

34 (a)
- May be required to do so by law   **4**
- To show how money has been spent
- Calculate the value of assets
- To make comparisons
- To calculate tax to be paid

  (b) (i)
- To increase the market share   **4**
- To reduce transport costs
- To take advantage of cheaper inputs
- To take advantage of Government grants
- To reach a global market

    (ii)
- May use up natural resources   **3**
- Force local companies out of business
- Profits may go back to home country

  (c) (i)
- Email   **3**
- Fax
- Video-conferencing
- Intranet
- Internet

    (ii)
- Fax – to send an exact copy of document to another branch   **3**
- Video-conferencing – to arrange meetings between countries without the need to travel
- Intranet – to convey information to all employees
- Internet – to reach more customers

  (d)
- Marketing – give advice on packaging, provide detailed plans for product updates   **6**
- Finance – find suppliers, work out budgets
- Human Resources – find employees, provide training

  (e)
- They affect the direction of the company   **2**
- They are made by owners or board of directors

(25)

Marks

35 *(a)*
- Owner – interested in the business making a profit and giving them a good return on their investment. They can show their interest by making decisions about the business and by investing more/less money into the business

- Employee – interested in job security and a good pay. They can show their interest by working well and providing a good service. They can also take industrial action if they are unhappy

- Customer – interested in receiving a good product/service at a good price. They can show their interest by recommending the business to friends/family or they can take their business elsewhere

- Suppliers – interested in getting repeat orders and getting paid for their orders. They can show their interest by refusing to supply goods or by offering/refusing to allow credit terms

- Government – interested to make sure the organisation is abiding by laws, paying the right amount of tax. The Government can show their interest by changing legislation or carrying out VAT inspections

10

(b)
- Oral – verbal information
- Written – information in the form of text
- Graphical – information in the form of charts and graphs
- Pictorial – information in the form of photographs
- Numerical – information in the form of numbers
- Quantitative – information that is expressed in figures
- Qualitative – information that is an expression that involves judgements/opinions

8

(c) (i) These are promotions offered by the retailer to the final customer to encourage them to buy the product/service

1

(ii)
- Free samples – where the customer is given a sample of the organisations products to encourage them to buy them in the future
- Demonstration – where the customer sees the product/service being used to encourage sales
- Competition – where the customer is entered into a competition once they buy the product/service
- Credit facilities – where customers are offered credit facilities to allow them to buy the product/service now and pay it later
- Buy one, get one free – customer receives two product/services but only pay for one
- Bonus packs – where the customer gains, e.g. 10% extra free
- Coupons/vouchers – where the customer is given money off coupons/vouchers to encourage sales

4

(d)
- Demonstration – where a member of staff watches the task being demonstrated by someone else, then tries it themselves (sometimes referred to as 'Sitting next to Nellie')
- Coaching – where the member of staff is taken through the task step by step and helped along the way
- Job rotation – where employees are moved around different jobs to learn different skills
- Distance learning – where a member of staff receives a training pack and works through this at their own pace, before sending it to an assessor for checking

2

(25)

Marks

36 *(a)* (i) • Age   **3**
- Gender
- Occupation
- Income
- Religion
- Geographical location
- Family lifestyle

(ii) • Purpose of questionnaire must be clearly stated   **4**
- Questionnaire should have a layout that is clear and easy to follow
- Questions should be relevant to purpose of the survey
- Questions should be short and to the point
- Questions should be in a logical order
- Question wording should be clear and simple

(b) • Can mean high storage costs and a large amount of space being taken up   **2**
- Money spent on stock could be used for something else
- Stock may deteriorate or go out of fashion

(c) • Sole trader: a business owned and controlled by one person. All profits are kept by   **6**
the owner and he/she is responsible for all decisions. A more personal service can be
offered. It is easy to set up. Owner has unlimited liability. Work ceases if owner is ill or
takes a holiday
- Partnership: a business owned by two or more people who own and control it. The
partners must produce a Partnership Agreement which states each partner's rights.
Partners can bring different areas of expertise to the business. Workload can be
shared as are profits. Partners have unlimited liability
- Private Limited Company: a business whose shares are owned privately. A minimum
of one shareholder is required to form this type of business. It is run by a director or
board of directors. There must be at least one director and one company secretary,
who is responsible for keeping the company records. The company has to produce a
Memorandum of Association and Articles of Association explaining details of the
company

(d) • Graphical: information in the form of graphs and charts. Could be used to display   **8**
monthly sales and make comparisons
- Oral: information in the form of sound. Used to make telephone calls and give
instructions to staff
- Pictorial: information in the form of pictures or photographs. Can be used to illustrate
certain points. Can also be used within text to make it more interesting
- Written: information in the form of words. Can be used to send letters, memos,
reports and emails

(e) • Employers must ensure that employees have a safe environment in which to work,   **2**
e.g. equipment checked and tested at regular intervals, hazardous substances dealt
with properly, staff trained and informed of potential dangers
- Employees are expected to behave in a reasonable manner at work and must take
responsibility for their own actions. They must ensure that all safety requirements are
met, follow instructions and undergo training when required

(25)

Marks

37 *(a)* (i) • Identifies target market 4
- Provides information on customer wants
- Indicates the potential size of the market
- Identifies what competitors are doing
- Provides information that helps develop correct advertising

(ii) • People may lie 5
- Sample size may be too small
- Market Researchers may not be trained
- Information may contain bias
- Information could become dated very quickly
- Poorly designed questionnaires
- Time taken may be too long

(b) • Suppliers – may raise their prices, change credit terms 8
- Employees – may reduce the quality of work, strike
- Managers – make decisions, motivate staff
- Customers – may stop buying

(c) • Primary – first-hand information collected for a specific purpose 8
- Secondary – second-hand information gathered for one purpose and re-used for another
- Internal – information created within the organisation
- External – information from outwith the organisation

(25)

38 *(a)* • Public Limited Company (plc) – a company that sells its shares on the stock market. A board of directors controls the company and the company must produce a Memorandum of Association and Articles of Association. Shareholders are the owners and get the chance to vote at the Annual General Meeting 4
- Private Limited Company (Ltd) – a company that sells its shares to friends and family only. A board of directors controls the company. The company must produce a Memorandum of Association and Articles of Association

(b) • Sales maximisation – to achieve as many sales as possible 4
- Profit maximisation – to achieve as much profit as possible
- Growth – to become larger, more competitive, able to take advantage of economies of sale
- Survival – to remain in business
- Managerial objectives – specific aims that the managers in the business have, e.g. to increase their own salary
- Social and ethical responsibility – to have a good public image/reputation

(c) • Line relationships – the relationships that exists between a manager and his/her subordinates 2
- Functional relationships – the relationships that exist between departments that provide specialist services

(d) (i) • The product/service being advertised 3
- The market segment the company is trying to target
- The budget available for advertising
- How competitors are advertising
- The size of the organisation
- Legal restrictions on advertising

Marks

(ii) Telephone survey – advantages
  • Relatively cheap to conduct
  • Responses are received immediately
  • A large number of people can be surveyed quickly

Telephone survey – disadvantages
  • Most people do not like answering questions to a stranger over the phone
  • Response rates can be poor as people put the phone down

Postal survey – advantage
  • Inexpensive as you do not need to have a trained interviewer

Postal survey – disadvantages
  • Questions must be straightforward for people to understand
  • Response rates are very low
  • Incentives may need to be offered to improve response rates

Hall test – advantage
  • Information gained from people is qualitative and includes their opinions/ judgements

Hall test – disadvantages
  • Qualitative information can be difficult to analyse
  • People may feel obliged to say good things about the product so information may not be entirely accurate

Personal interview – advantages
  • Allows for two-way communication to take place
  • Interviewers can clear up any misunderstandings
  • Interviewers can encourage respondents

Personal interview – disadvantages
  • Can be expensive to hire and train researchers
  • People do not like being interviewed in their home/stopped in the street for their opinion

8

(e) • Flat rate – employees are paid a set salary, divided into 12 monthly payments
  • Piece rate – employees are paid for each item they produce
  • Time rate – employees are paid for each hour they work
  • Overtime – employees are paid more than their usual hourly rate for extra hours they work
  • Bonus rate – employees are paid a basic salary, but gain an additional payment if they meet specific targets
  • Commission – employees are paid a basic salary and a percentage of the sales value

4

(25)

39 (a) • Trade credit: a business buys goods from suppliers and pays for them at a later date
  • Mortgage: a loan payable over a long number of years, usually given for the purchase of property; interest is charged
  • Retained profit: profit kept from previous years

3

(b) • External information: information from sources outside an organisation
  • Examples: information from government statistics, market research, newspapers and competitors

4

(c) (i) • 'Into the pipeline' promotions: promotions offered by manufacturers to retailers to encourage them to stock their goods
      • 'Out of the pipeline' promotions: promotions offered by retailers to customers to encourage them to buy their goods

2

  (ii) • Into the pipeline examples: point of sale displays; sale or return; dealer competitions; credit facilities; staff training
      • Out of the pipeline examples: free samples; demonstrations; buy one get one free; bonus packs; free offers

4

(d) • Managers: check how profitable the organisation is; identify areas where savings could be made and costs reduced. If organisation is making good profits, manager may expect to get bonus
  • Potential investors: if organisation is making good profits they will be inclined to invest in it as they can expect a healthy return for their investment
  • Banks: if organisation is profitable they can expect to get back any monies borrowed. If organisation is unprofitable they will not be inclined to give further loans
  • Inland Revenue: the more profit an organisation makes, the more tax the Inland Revenue can charge
  • Suppliers: if organisation is profitable they can expect prompt payment for their supplies and also further orders

5

(e) • Coaching: a trainee is shown the task step by step
  • Job rotation: a trainee moves around different departments learning different tasks in each
  • Distance learning: a trainee receives a pack of materials to work through at their own pace. When completed it is sent back to be assessed and evaluated

3

(f) • Application forms are checked against the person specification
  • Suitable candidates are called for interview
  • Tests may be carried out, e.g. attainment tests, IQ tests, aptitude tests
  • References checked
  • Best candidate is selected and offered position
  • Once position is accepted, unsuccessful candidates are informed

4

40 (a) • Political factors: Government may impose certain laws which organisations must comply with or face prosecution. To comply with the laws, organisations may have to change certain things which could result in much expense for the organisation
  • Economic factors: An increase in interest rates could affect the organisation as this results in paying more for money borrowed from banks
  • Social factors: Changes in peoples' tastes affect organisations as they have to adjust their products to meet changing tastes
  • Technological factors: Organisations must keep up with new technological advances. If not, they face losing customers and as a result sales and profits will decrease
  • Environmental facts: Storms, floods and pollution affect organisations. Organisations affected by any of these often have to close for long periods of time which results in lost sales and profits are affected

8

(b) • Change the packaging   • Change the price   • Change the ingredients
  • Change channels of distribution

3

(c) • To identify training needs   • To identify employees who are ready for promotion
  • To set targets for employees   • To identify any problems employees may be experiencing   • To identify strengths and weaknesses and address these
  • To improve communication   • To motivate staff
  • To award increases in salary

4

Marks

(d) Primary   **6**

- Advantage: information is first hand and therefore has more chance of being correct
- Disadvantage: market research costs may be high. Sample may be too small, therefore sample may not take in a wide area of view. Those questioned may not be telling the truth

Secondary

- Advantage: inexpensive and easy to collect. Wide variety of sources available
- Disadvantage: information gathered has been used before and may be out of date. It is also available to competitors

Internal

- Advantage: information should be accurate as it is coming from your own organisation
- Disadvantage: accurate records have to be kept in order for information to be of any use

(e) Public sector organisation   **4**

- To meet the needs of the local people
- To provide a wide range of services
- To stick to agreed budgets
- To break even

Charity

- To provide a service to the needy
- To relieve poverty
- To fund research

(25)

41 (a) Cash flow problems   **6**

- Too much money tied up in stock
- Customers being given too much time to pay
- Customers being given too much credit
- High borrowing and interest rates
- Owner taking too many drawings
- Low sales
- Purchase of capital items

Resolution to cash flow problems

- Offer discounts and promotions to encourage sales
- Sell unnecessary fixed assets
- Arrange credit facilities with suppliers
- Owner takes fewer drawings
- Buy capital items on hire purchase
- Encourage debtors to pay
- Source another method of finance – e.g. float on stock exchange, take on a partner

(b)
- Employees – interested to ensure they are getting a fair pay deal from the organisation and to ensure job security   **4**
- Suppliers – interested in the liquidity of an organisation to ensure the organisation will be able to pay its debt and will continue to give the creditor custom
- Bank – interested in ensuring the business is able to pay back any loan the bank has given

- Local community – interested in the business being successful to ensure jobs are available within the community

(c) (i) Organisation – advantages   **8**
  - Increased productivity
  - Reduced waste/error
  - More consistent quality
  - Reduced labour costs
  - ICT can operate 24 hours, seven days a week without the need for breaks
  - Improved communication
  - Faster decision making possible

  Organisation – disadvantages
  - Costly to install and maintain
  - If a breakdown occurs, production may need to stop
  - Data can become corrupt due to a virus

  Employee – advantages
  - Staff will gain additional skills
  - Staff will receive training in how to operate the ICT
  - Improved communication
  - Improved working conditions as fewer accidents occur with ICT

  Employee – disadvantages
  - Staff may lose jobs
  - Staff may feel demotivated/de-skilled
  - Staff may not feel comfortable with the training and working the ICT

(ii) Spreadsheet package – e.g. Microsoft Excel – but also accept database or word processing packages   **1**

(d) (i) • Manufacturer to consumer   • Manufacturer to wholesaler to consumer   **3**
  - Manufacturer to wholesaler to retailer to consumer

(ii) • Product being sold   • Reliability of companies in the channel of distribution   **3**
  - Finance available to the organisation   • Government restrictions
  - Stage in the product life cycle   • Desired image for the product
  - Manufacturer's capacity to distribute

(25)

42 *(a)* • To highlight periods when a negative cash/bank balance is expected so that finance can be arranged in advance to remedy this   **3**
  - To forecast when extra cash may be available as it may allow the firm to invest in assets for the future
  - If future overspending is expected, then corrective action can be taken to cover this

(b) (i) • Quality Assurance: at certain points during the production process, products are checked to ensure they meet certain standards. Unacceptable products are then discarded   **6**
  - Total Quality Management: a system of doing things right first time. All staff in the organisation are involved in ensuring absolute quality of their work and no errors are tolerated
  - Quality Circles: small groups of workers meet at regular intervals to discuss how improvements can be made. Suggestions are then made to senior management

Marks

- Benchmarking: copying the methods used by another organisation that has been recognised as the 'best'

(ii) • Job production • Batch production • Flow production   **3**

(iii) • Job production – wedding dress; specially designed piece of furniture   **3**
- Batch production – bread rolls, tins of soup
- Flow production – cars, television sets

(c) (i) • Centralised structure: control and decision making made by senior management   **2**
- Decentralised structure: control and decision making delegated to departments within the organisation

(ii) Centralise structure – advantages   **4**
- Procedures are standardised
- Decisions can be made for whole organisation

Centralised structure – disadvantages
- Staff have very little scope to show their initiative and may become frustrated as a result

Decentralised structure – advantages
- Staff become more motivated as they are given more responsibility
- Senior management are relieved of many routine tasks

Decentralised structure – disadvantages
- Inexperienced managers may make wrong decisions which could be costly to organisation

(d) Costs   **4**
- Staff may use it for personal use, thus incurring heavy costs for organisation
- It can be time consuming accessing suitable information owing to the large amount available

Benefits
- Allows organisations to advertise and sell their products world-wide.
- Allows organisation to check information on competitors and also new products coming on to market

(25)

43 *(a)* (i) • Television • Radio • Billboards • Magazine/newspaper   **3**
- Mail shots

(ii) • Cost • Target audience – who and how many • What competitors use   **3**

(b) • Identify the problem • Identify a number of possible solutions   **5**
- Decide on the best solution • Communicate the decision
- Implement the decision • Evaluate the decision

(c) • Well lit • Secure • Well ventilated • Dry • Clearly labelled   **5**
- Stock rotation system • Heavy items at low level

(d) (i) Hierarchical structure – a structure with many levels of management   **1**

(ii) Costs   **4**
- Information may become lost
- Information may become distorted
- Wages bill will be high
- Decision making will take longer

Benefits
- Clearly defined roles
- Small span of control
- Specialisation

(iii)
- Flat structure – an organisational structure with few levels of management
- Matrix structure – a team made up of employees from different departments

4

(25)

44 *(a)* (i)
- Focus group – selecting a group of people who will sit together and discuss product/service
- Telephone survey – market researcher phones people in their home and asks them questions
- Postal survey – market researcher sends out a questionnaire to people through the post
- Consumer audit – where larger organisations carry out continuous research to monitor buying habits and influences on consumers
- Hall test – where consumers are invited to try out a product and give their reactions to it
- Personal interview – a face-to-face interview which could be held in the street or in someone's home

6

(ii) Focus group – advantage
- Qualitative information on people's opinions/judgements can be gained

6

Focus group – disadvantage
- Difficult to analyse this type of information

Telephone survey – advantages
- Relatively cheap to conduct
- Responses are received immediately
- A large number of people can be surveyed quickly

Telephone survey – disadvantage
- Most people do not like answering questions to a stranger over the phone
- Response rates can be poor as people put the phone down

Postal survey – advantage
- Inexpensive as you do not need to have a trained interviewer

Postal survey – disadvantages
- Questions must be straightforward for people to understand
- Response rates are very low
- Incentives may need to be offered to improve response rates

Consumer audit – advantages
- Accurate information can be gained if consumers keep the diary up-to-date
- Information gained can often indicate consumer trends

Consumer audit – disadvantages
- Expensive as consumers need to be paid to do this
- Often consumers drop out part-way through the process
- Diaries can often be incomplete

Hall test – advantage
- Information gained from people is qualitative and includes their opinions/judgements

Marks

Hall test – disadvantages
- Qualitative information can be difficult to analyse
- People may feel obliged to say good things about the product so information may not be entirely accurate

Personal interview – advantages
- Allows for two-way communication to take place
- Interviewers can clear up any misunderstandings
- Interviewers can encourage respondents

Personal interview – disadvantages
- Can be expensive to hire and train researchers
- People do not like being interviewed in their home/stopped in the street for their opinion

(b)
- Flat rate – employees are paid a set salary, divided into 12 monthly payments
- Piece rate – employees are paid for each item they produce
- Time rate – employees are paid for each hour they work
- Overtime – employees are paid more than their usual hourly rate for extra hours they work
- Bonus rate – employees are paid a basic salary, but gain an additional payment if they meet specific targets
- Commission – employees are paid a basic salary and a percentage of the sales value

8

(c) (i)
- Availability of labour in terms of skill and costs
- Technology available
- Type of product being produced
- Quantity of product being produced

1

(ii) Labour-intensive – advantages
- Product is hand-crafted, so the price can be more expensive
- Individual customer requirements can be catered for
- Staff are more motivated as jobs can be different

4

Labour intensive – disadvantages
- Highly skilled employees can be expensive to hire
- Levels of output may be small
- If staff are absent, production may need to stop
- Quality of output has to be monitored closely

Capital intensive – advantages
- Product is made to a standard level at all times
- Machinery can work 24 hours, seven days without needing breaks
- Machinery can produce high numbers in a short period of time
- Can be helpful when labour costs are high

Capital intensive – disadvantages
- Can be costly to install and maintain machinery
- If breakdowns occur, production may have to stop
- Individual, one-off jobs cannot be easily catered for
- Employees find it a boring job – less motivated

(25)

Marks

45 *(a)* (i) • Just-in-time stock control – keeping stock levels to a minimum, thus reducing costs. Stock arrives just in time to be used in production. Goods are not produced unless a firm order has been received from a customer   **1**

(ii) Advantages   **4**
- Money is not tied up in stock   • Less storage space is required
- Deterioration of stock is reduced   • Less chance of products going out of fashion

Disadvantages
- Highly dependent on reliable suppliers
- If stock is late in arriving, production is in danger of being disrupted
- May lose discounts if not buying in bulk
- Increased administration costs due to ordering as and when stock required

(b) (i) • The cost of providing the service (e.g. labour, materials used, expenses)   **3**
- Suppliers' prices   • Competitors' prices   • Profit level expected
- Place where business is located   • State of economy

(ii) • Advertise in local paper/local radio /internet   • Give out vouchers   **2**
- Competitions   • Special offers

(c) Desk research: carried out at a person's desk using secondary information from published sources   **2**

Field research: carried out outside in order to obtain first-hand information

(d) • Aptitude tests: assess the natural ability of candidates to carry out certain tasks   **3**
- Intelligent tests: assess the mental ability of a candidate
- Psychometric tests: assess a candidate's responses to questions, analysed to reveal their personality and traits
- Medical/fitness tests: assess a person's medical condition before offering a position

(e) • Marketing: selling goods and services, advertising and promotion   **6**
- Finance: keeping financial records, controlling money, preparing budgets and financial statements
- Operations: responsible for the production of goods/services, selecting the best suppliers, storing, distribution and delivery of goods
- Human Resources: responsible for managing staff, recruitment, staff training, maintaining employee records
- Administration: provides office support, health and safety issues, layout and design

(f) • Accurate   • Timely   • Complete   • Relevant   • Free from bias   **4**
- Appropriate   • High quality

(25)